DOLL-MAKING
from Modern Craft Clays

DOLL-MAKING
from Modern Craft Clays

Patience Kornicka

Dryad Press Ltd London

Acknowledgement

I would like to thank Worthing Museum for the loan of their antique doll's furniture used in some of the colour photographs, and Dr Sally White for her enthusiastic assistance in this respect. Thank you also to my husband for his support and encouragement.

Photographs by
Steve Forrest
Elmcroft Studios
Findon, West Sussex
Drawings and diagrams by the author

ISBN 0 8521 9667 9

Typeset by Progress Filmsetting Ltd
and printed in Great Britain by
Anchor Brendon Ltd
Tiptree Essex
for the publishers
Dryad Press Ltd.
4 Fitzhardinge Street
London W1H 0AH

Contents

Introduction

It is very rare for anything completely original to appear on the fashion scene. Trends in clothes tend to revolve around established themes and derive a great deal of inspiration from the styles of previous generations.

A fashion in playthings can also become a pendulum, harking back to the past, as is beginning to happen now. Over the last 25 years it appeared that plastic had established itself as the new material for all toys, dolls in particular. It seemed that the days of Hornby trains, metal Meccano, lead soldiers etc. were long gone. Dolls changed from being small cherished porcelain images of their owners to become inelegant mass-produced and stereotyped. They wailed, winked and wetted, and became ever more mechanical in their capabilities. Clothes were machine-made and more or less identical to all the others on the market. The individual charm of dolls dressed lovingly by mothers was gone, as was the originality of former years. But now the wheel has turned a full circle and reproduction dolls are once again all the rage. The German doll industry in particular, has revived and some of the lovely porcelain dolls created from the same moulds as used at the beginning of this century are now being sold at high prices. Antique dolls, if genuine, can command even higher prices. Courses on making reproduction dolls are now numerous but this method of doll-making is costly for the beginner as it requires expensive materials such as high-grade slip, and a kiln to fire the dolls. The dolls, if successful, then require cloth bodies and dressing in the relevant period attire. This requires an added skill—in designing paper patterns and a knowledge of period costume, or of the places and books where it may be found. Clothes for hand-sewn dolls cannot be made in the same way as the modern machine-made ones. Old skills have to be re-learned.

Some fortunate people searching in the attics of their childhood homes have rediscovered some of their original dolls, or better still, the dolls of their parents or grand-parents. This may prove to be a very valuable find, for dolls can now be repaired with doll parts that match the originals and there are numerous doll-repair shops throughout the country.

After the war, and many years in the A.T.S., I returned briefly, to the house of my childhood, and searched in the attic and cellar for my dolls and doll's house. An incendiary bomb in the cellar had caused my doll's house, amongst other things, to disappear and the attic revealed only a few moth-eaten items of doll's clothing, lovingly sewn by my mother, which had included knitted baby clothes and a copy of my school uniform for a child doll. Gone too, were one or two lovely dolls; a working steam-engine to pull Hornby 0 gauge railway carriages; an incredible American metal building kit for sky-scraper buildings, etc. Not a lot of encouragement there. Perhaps that is why, some 35 years later, I have recreated a collection of dolls and a doll's house.

If you have no genuine antique dolls of your own and cannot afford to start collecting them, what are the alternatives? If you plan to attend a course on making reproduction dolls it must be remembered that without a kiln you can make only the dolls produced on the course and if a kiln is purchased, a sales outlet will be required to sell the surplus dolls. Another alternative is to buy some of those doll reproductions in kit form. There are a number to choose from, obtained from craft suppliers by post or from the Victoria and Albert Museum where a small stock is held.

In my opinion the most exciting alternative is to make a unique doll collection, which can be done inexpensively from self-hardening clay or domestic oven-baked clay. Each doll will be your own creation and each one will be totally different from its fellows and from anybody else's origination. The dolls may represent any race and colour; Chinese, African, Indian, etc., with hair style and colour to complement the choice. The dolls can be of any age group and life-style, they can be baby dolls, child dolls, teenagers, adult dolls, elderly dolls, character dolls, etc. The best dolls may well become family heirlooms. Dolls can also be a very effective souvenir of a happy holiday, dressed in the appropriate folk costume—so much better than the plastic imitations sold at holiday resorts. And of course, as originally intended, dolls can be playthings; once painted and varnished these dolls will not deteriorate and are robust and sturdy enough to withstand normal play.

=ONE=

Construction of the dolls

There are a number of skills which must be mastered when making dolls from clay: forming a head and limbs from craft clay; making a body section from a pattern and stuffing it correctly; painting the face; making a wig; and, finally, dressing the doll according to chosen style.

Making a head

Most of the equipment required can be found around the home.

Modelling tools:
cocktail sticks
tooth picks
cotton buds
a penknife or butter knife
salt spoon
For the modelling platform:
a block of wood about 3 cm (1¼ in.) thick and measuring not less than 15 x 10 cm (6 x 4 in.)
1 sock knitting needle (points at both ends)
a length of crêpe paper
kitchen foil or cling film
a length of dowel 2½ cm (1 in.) in diameter and 7½ cm (3 in.) long
For the head;
a polystyrene ball 5 cm (2 in.) in diameter
a packet of self-drying clay — Das is used in this book (as a guide, a large packet will make about three adult heads or four baby/child doll heads)
plastic bag and cleaning rag
mist sprayer and bowl of water
a rolling pin and board

To make the modelling stand

Prepare the piece of dowel by flattening one rounded side to enable it to rest on a flat surface, remove about one third of the side; this can be achieved by placing the dowel in a vice and using a plane or wood scraper. Glue this shoulder support to the wooden base with strong wood glue and leave to dry. When dry, drill a hole through the centre of the dowel and half way through the base block to accommodate the knitting needle. See diagrams 1 and 2. (The shaded area in the second diagram refers to adult heads.) Press the polystyrene ball onto the knitting needle exactly through the middle but leave a 4-5 cm space below for the neck. A baby doll will have a shorter neck than a child doll. Cover the curved shoulder of dowel with foil or cling film to prevent the wet clay sticking to the surface. Cut a piece of crêpe paper 22 cm (9 in.) long by about 7-8 cm (2¾-3¼ in.); flute the edges and wind around the needle showing beneath the ball, fasten with glue or sellotape. The crêpe paper provides a good base on which to shape the neck (diagram 3). Everything is now ready for modelling.

Take a substantial amount of clay from the packet but be sure to reseal the packet to keep the remainder fresh. Knead the clay well to remove any air bubbles. Place on a board and, with a rolling pin, roll out to a thickness of about ½ cm (¼ in.). Trim the piece (as in pastry-making) to a circle sufficiently large to cover all the polystyrene ball. Push it over the knitting needle (diagram 4) and cut sections of

9

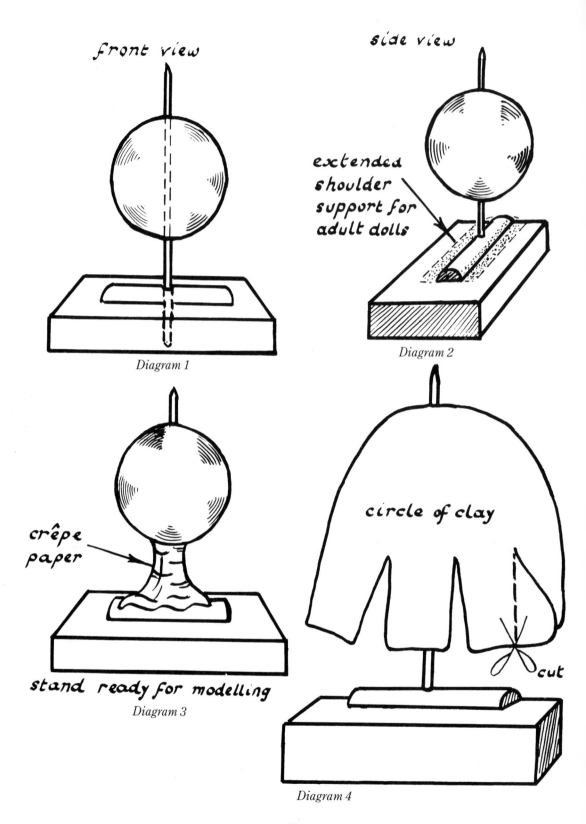

front view

Diagram 1

side view

extended
shoulder
support for
adult dolls

Diagram 2

crêpe
paper

stand ready for modelling

Diagram 3

circle of clay

cut

Diagram 4

clay off with scissors, enabling the clay to fit smoothly over the ball. This is best achieved by pressing the clay smoothly over the ball and making folds of spare clay which stick out. Cut the spare clay off close to the head, this leaves a ball that is completely covered with clay but with no overlaps. Moisten the ball with a water-filled mist sprayer and then smooth the surface and joins, eradicating any bumps. Roll a strip of clay, the same thickness as for the head (about 5 x 8 cm (2 x 3¼ in.)), for the neck. Wrap it around and over the crêpe paper, sealing the ends and where it joins the head. Spray constantly to keep the clay moist. A third piece of clay of the same thickness is required for the shoulders. Cut out a circle about 7½-8 cm (3-3¼ in.) in diameter and cut across the middle; place each semi-circle over the dowel and to the front and back of the head. Spray, seal and smooth the edges of all the joins. With a cocktail stick make four holes, two to the front and two to the back. The holes must always be kept open as they are necessary for sewing the head to the cloth body.

The next stage is modelling the features of the face. A live model would be ideal but it is unlikely that any child would be willing to sit still for hours on end so alternatives need to be found. A good photograph is one answer, another is a book on drawing portraits. A head that is shown full-face, three-quarters and profile will provide a guide for the modeller at every stage (diagram 5). The ears are level with the eyes and both are halfway down the head. The space between the eyes is usually the width of an eye.

Roll a sausage of clay, about finger size, for the forehead and another for the chin. Press the clay to the head, tapering the ends away until they disappear completely. Fingers, cotton buds, or other tools may be helpful in holding the clay firmly together. Check the profile, the brow may recede or the chin appear concave, add further clay as required. The head should be egg-shaped so squeeze the sides of the head between the palms of the hands until the clay is pressed thinner at the sides. At the same time the back of the head may be too flat. Take a

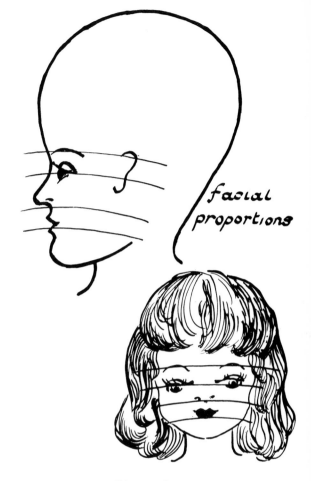

Diagram 5

piece of clay about the size of half a walnut and place high at the back of the head diagonally opposite the chin, and work it into the surrounding clay. Check the profile again and keep the clay moist.

All errors can be rectified, do not be afraid to cut off lumps of clay or add extra elsewhere. A pause in modelling may be beneficial—cover the dampened head with a plastic bag and leave overnight; it will not deteriorate and it is surprising how a fresh look after a period of time gives new insight into errors. When recommencing work look at the head from all angles: from the top of the head, from the back, in a mirror—faults will appear as if by magic! Correct them before attempting to add cheeks, nose, eyes, mouth and ears.

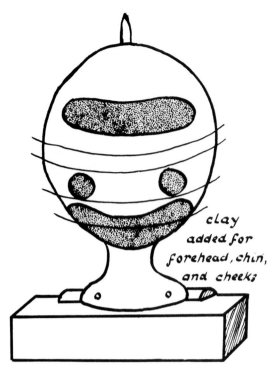

Diagram 6

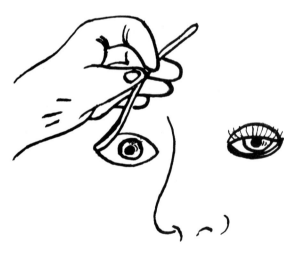

clay
added for
forehead, chin,
and cheeks

method for inserting
glass eyes, adding
clay strip surround

Diagram 7

For the cheeks add marbles of clay (diagram 6) and work them in. Check the position is correct, not too far round towards the ears, not too far to the front. Cheeks for a baby or young child will be placed lower than for an adult.

For the nose take a morsel of clay and shape into a triangle. As an aid to placing the features, scratch guide lines for the position of eyes, nose and mouth onto the clay—they can easily be erased later. Attach the nose by the point of the top triangle and pinch in with the fingers, press to the surrounding clay with a cotton bud. Shape the nose; a baby's nose will tend to be uptilted and button-shaped but a child's will be narrower and more defined. Keep the features moist at all times. Check the profile for angle and shape. Gouge out nostrils with a cocktail-stick and, at the same time, bring out the sides of the nose.

For the eye sockets rotate the ball of a finger on the eye line which will also raise the area above the eye line and produce a slight eyebrow overhang. Take a very tiny morsel of clay between finger and thumb and form into an oval and place in the eye socket. Alternatively, a flat-backed eye can be obtained from doll suppliers but care must be taken to ensure it is the correct size for the doll (diagram 7). The eye must be pressed well into the eye socket or a pop-eyed look will result. Painted eyes can be just as attractive and are best for first attempts.

For the mouth take another tiny morsel of clay and attach with gentle pressure. To give depth to the mouth cavity, very delicately insert the tip of a knife between the lips and rotate a cocktail stick within the mouth, then close the mouth again or leave slightly parted lips. Shape the lips with the tip of the cocktail stick and with very delicate movements lift the bow of the lips and ease in the dimpled corners of the mouth.

To make the ears attach two small shells of clay on the ear line by the front of the shell and leave free at the rear. Press with a cotton bud to produce the ear cavity and lobe.

For the hair see instructions on how to make a wig, page 21. For a baby doll, roll out wafer thin pieces of clay and attach them to the hair line of the baby's head, pressing with cotton buds. Continue with separate pieces until the whole scalp is covered where a baby's hair normally grows. Spray, then make swirling movements with a cocktail stick or tiny comb to resemble waves and curls. It is even possible to form small clay curls wound round a cocktail stick and attach these, at one end, to the head. Only a few curls should be attempted as they are fragile and will not survive long if the doll is to be a plaything.

Finally, before leaving the head to dry out, spray again with a mist sprayer as this will help smooth away any uneven surfaces and reduce the amount of sanding necessary. If not completely satisfied with the head, cover with a plastic bag and reconsider later. This can be very helpful as, after a period of hours, the clay changes consistency and becomes a whole substance rather than an amalgamation of numerous pieces. Once the clay has changed to this state experiments can be made in changing the expression of the face. The face can be given a 'face lift' in much the same way as a human face. The mouth can be made happier by gentle pressure on the spot where the jaw bone should be. The chin can be brought out and the face made less round, all with an experienced squeeze here and another there.

The completed head is now left to dry out naturally. After several days the head can be removed from the stand and the knitting needle withdrawn with pincers, the head will then dry out further from beneath. After removing the needle the hole in the top of the head can be filled with fresh clay. If the shoulders seem too frail, reinforce them with added clay. Patching can still be done at this stage as any join marks can be removed with sandpaper. It is wise to leave the head for about a week before sanding; only the finest grade of sandpaper should be used. Tear off tiny pieces and wrap around a cocktail stick and smooth the sides of the nose and around the eyes, chin and brow. A double fold of sandpaper will suffice to smooth the lips and the bow can be emphasised, the lower lip softened, and so

forth. Sometimes it is only when dry that faults become apparent. Do not be afraid, take a hobby file and file away! The rough edges will have to be smoothed back to a pristine state with a good deal of sanding. A roll of sandpaper will smooth the neck and shoulders. Ensure that the lower edges of the shoulders are smooth where they join the body, if too thick and heavy it will be difficult to attach them to the body, a file will angle the edges.

Painting the face

Poster colours are used to paint the face, and both a coarse and a fine brush will be required along with a can of artist's fixative. Alternatively, the head can be varnished for a more glossy look but the spray is preferable as it is difficult not to leave some brush strokes. It will leave a matt egg-shell finish that is pleasing in appearance and touch. First, paint the whole head all over with flesh-coloured paint, two coats will be necessary for density of colour penetration. Mix the paint with as little water as possible and only enough to aid application. If brush marks remain use a light pressure of mist sprayer. Flesh colour can be made from mixing white with a touch of vermillion and a little yellow. Alternatively it can be bought ready-mixed. The colour is often too ruddy for a delicate doll but can be softened with added white. The first coat of paint makes a great difference to the head and the colour tends to highlight any errors that might not have been visible before. Edges that are too sharp will be very apparent and can be corrected even now. Sand away any imperfections even if it removes paint as well as clay. Touch up and apply the second coat of paint.

Next comes shading. A painting pad is useful here and can be used again and again if washed. Ideally it should be made of pure silk but fine lawn may suffice. Cut a piece of fabric the size of a small handkerchief and place a square of cotton wool in the centre. Make a parcel of the padding by wrapping over all edges of the fabric and stitching it up in order to prevent unravelling when wrung out. Alternatively, use a small real sponge (cosmetic variety) obtainable from chemists. Mix a small quantity of cheek shading slightly darker than the flesh tint but with a touch of rose. Take care not to make the colour too dark as it will look unnatural and will be deepened when varnish is applied. Wring out the painting pad in clean water and dip one side into the cheek colouring then apply in light dabs to cheek area. Turn the pad over and dab away any strong colour edges. Repeat the process for eye shading, using soft pastel shades of blue, grey, or green mixed with white. Using a fine brush take a little of the cheek colour and apply to the inside of the nostrils and corners of the mouth. Using a fine brush, paint in the entire almond shape of the eye with white paint. Two coats will be necessary. When quite dry, paint the iris of the eye. For blue eyes mix blue with white and for brown eyes use ready-mixed brown, or black, red and yellow. As the iris will be later covered with nail polish for lustre, make sure the colours are clear and bright. When dry, paint the pupil of the eye with black paint. Make sure that the iris and pupil are not too small, preferably even a little over-sized; it is all too easy to achieve 'piggy' eyes if both are too small. Apply a coat of nail polish to the iris, either transparent or coloured blue or brown. Re-apply a touch of black to the pupil over the dried nail polish. For a final touch, apply a fleck of white to highlight the eye, also a hint of pink at the corner of the eyes. With flesh-coloured paint, paint in the eyelids, a wide-eyed look for dolls is attractive, or a sleepy look for a baby doll. Outline the white area of the eye with a touch of shadow applied with a fine brush. With the finest brush available paint in a few eyelashes with light brown paint, just a few curving strokes. At the same time paint a delicate eyebrow arch, using a pencilled line as a guide. Do not place the eyebrows too high or the doll will appear perpetually surprised! A demure look for a shy young girl doll can be emphasised with slightly downcast eyes and eye lashes down-turned.

For the lips use the remainder of the cheek shadow, deepening the colour only slightly

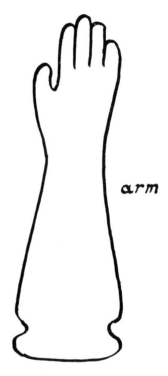

arm

Diagram 8

with the merest touch of rose. Outline the lips, then fill in the remainder.

Preserve your doll's face with colourless artist's fixative or a coat of semi-gloss varnish.

Making the limbs

Arms

These can be made from the same self-drying clay as used for the head. Take a piece of well-kneaded and well-moistened clay and roll into a sausage about the diameter of a finger and 7-8 cm (3¼-3½ in.) in length. At a distance of about 3 cm (1¼ in.) from the lower end of the arm, roll the wrist between finger and thumb and apply even pressure all round the doll's arm. To shape the hand flatten the clay and remove a segment of clay between thumb and fingers with scissors. Roll the thumb to shape and define separation of the fingers with a cocktail stick. Do not separate the fingers as

14

the clay might break when dry. Check the length of the thumb and fingers and remove any surplus. With a cocktail stick make a deep indentation all round the upper arm at a distance of about ½ cm (¼ in.) from the elbow; the recess shown should be deep enough to take several layers of thread when sewing to the calico arm. Leave the arms to dry out thoroughly, this can take longer than the head due to the density of clay. A second arm is made to match the first but take care to make a left and a right hand. Bring the thumb in a little towards the palm for added realism. When completely dry paint the arm with two coats of flesh colour and leave to dry in an upright position or suspend by a thread from a convenient shelf. Complete with a coat of varnish or spray fixative and apply pink nail polish to the ends of the fingers.

Alternatively, very attractive arms can be made from domestic oven-baked clay called Fimo, obtainable from craft shops and suppliers. The clay is produced in a wide range of colours, one of which is flesh. The colour is just right for limbs and needs no other treatment, such as painting or varnishing, when modelling is complete. The clay might seem more costly but the advantages are numerous and a large packet containing four separate blocks will make a number of adult or child doll limbs. Experiment with the smaller size to begin with and move to the larger size if satisfied with the result. The main advantage is texture and strength. It is 'fired' in a normal, domestic oven at a temperature of 130°C (268°F) for ten to 20 minutes. After which time it is hard and permanent. Unlike self-drying clay, the fingers of hands can be individually moulded and moved in a variety of natural postures. Fingers can be curved to hold baskets, parasols, etc.

If using this type of clay it is necessary to understand that it should be handled differently. When taken from the packet it will break off and crumble and appear rather useless, but its texture changes totally when handled and well-kneaded. After a considerable amount of hand massaging the texture changes to that closely resembling plasticine and has all the advantages of plasticine—plus permanence. Shape the arm as for Das clay. The palm of the hand is hollowed out with a cotton bud. Flatten the hand slightly, remove the triangle between finger and thumb with scissors. Bring in the thumb joint over the palm (examine your own hand) and separate all fingers with scissors. Treat each finger separately, rolling and shaping and removing the surplus at the tips as this process elongates the fingers. Curve the fingers slightly; study the natural and relaxed position of a child's hand. Fimo clay remains constantly pliable until it is baked and requires no moisture. Once baked it cannot be altered so ensure that the limb is exactly right before firing. Lay the limb on a baking sheet in its correct position, taking care to ensure that it cannot fall over during baking. Fire the limb for a test ten minutes, then a further ten minutes if required. No painting or varnishing is required but the nails may still be painted with pink nail polish.

Legs

Take a well-kneaded and well moistened piece of clay and roll to a fatter sausage than for the arms, the overall length being about 9 cm (3½ in.). Bend the sausage at the ankle leaving a foot size of about 3½ cm (2 in.). Shape the ankle with a rolling pressure and curve the leg very slightly, pushing out a calf at the back and smoothing the front of the leg. Study a human leg and endeavour to copy the shape (diagram 9). Flatten the bottom of the foot, shape the instep and round the toes to a gradual point. Check the length of the foot and trim back to 3½ cm (2 in.). Pull out the heel slightly. Stand the leg upright and check the overall dimensions. A leg length of 7-8 cm (2¾-3¼ in.) from the top of the leg to standing surface will be about correct for a doll measuring some 30-31 cm (12-12½ in.) tall. Cut off any surplus leg at the knee and make an indentation all round the leg with cocktail stick, as described for the arms. Make a second leg in the same way, taking care to make a right and a left leg. Paint and varnish as for arms.

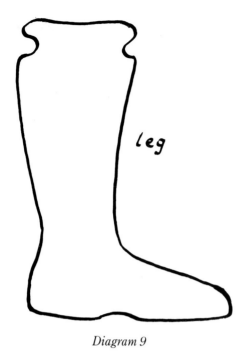

Diagram 9

Alternatively, make the legs from Fimo clay in flesh colour as described for the arms. The 'fired' appearance of such limbs is remarkably like that of shop-bought dolls.

Bodies

Use unbleached calico for the bodies and a good quality filling such as pure kapok or cellulose filling.

For a child doll trace the patterns shown on diagrams 10 and 14; one front body, two back bodies, four legs and two arms. Pin the patterns to the calico, observing any instructions. Cut out the pieces carefully with sharp scissors. Use a sewing machine for the bodies, if possible. Close the darts on the back pieces and stitch, leaving the neck open for the filling. With a small stitch, zig-zag all round the seams, or oversew. Pin the front section to the backs, right sides together, stitch and zig-zag, easing in any fullness. Pin the two leg pieces together and stitch and zig-zag side seams. Repeat for second leg. Fold the arms over and stitch and zig-zag the side seam.

Stuffing

Stuff the body firmly with very small pieces of filling, one piece at a time, continually pressing the filling down into the corners of the hips with a wooden spoon handle. Shape the seat area to a pleasant round shape and continue stuffing to the waist, taking care to stuff the waist firmly. Continue stuffing to the shoulders and neck. The filling will tend to shrink and is best left overnight before closing the neck. It is most likely that further stuffing will be necessary for a firm, but not over-stuffed, body.

Stuffing the arms Following diagram 11, place the arm, inverted, into the calico arm with the wrong side outside. Thread a needle with strong button thread and run a gathering thread all round the top of the calico arm and draw up to fit the groove in the clay arm, then wind several lengths around the arm and fasten off. Turn the calico arm right side out and check the position of the hand in relation to the seams on the arm. Commence stuffing to the elbow only. With beige thread, stitch across the arm as indicated. Continue stuffing to the shoulder, then stitch across again. The arm is now capable of natural movements. Put to one side and complete the other arm in the same way. Stitch to the body, taking care to stitch the right arm to the right side and the left arm to the left. Turn in raw edges and stitch to the body with strong thread.

Stuffing the legs Following diagram 12, complete the legs as for the arms. Take care to have the right and left feet in the correct positions. Take particular care to stuff the legs firmly as they have to support the weight of the whole doll. Stitch at the knee and hip as with the elbow and shoulder of the arms. Open out the raw edges to the leg and fold under, pin the legs in position with the front leg placed well up on the hip and the back leg pinned to the seat of the doll. Check sufficient movement is left for the doll to be able to sit and stand up. Stitch with strong thread.

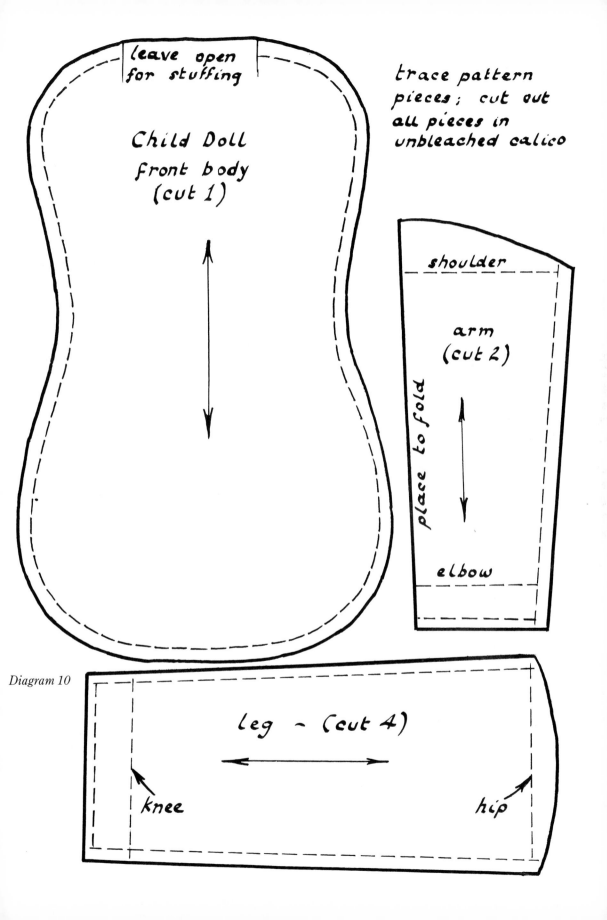

leave open
for stuffing

trace pattern
pieces; cut out
all pieces in
unbleached calico

Child Doll
front body
(cut 1)

shoulder

arm
(cut 2)

place to fold

elbow

Diagram 10

leg - (cut 4)

knee

hip

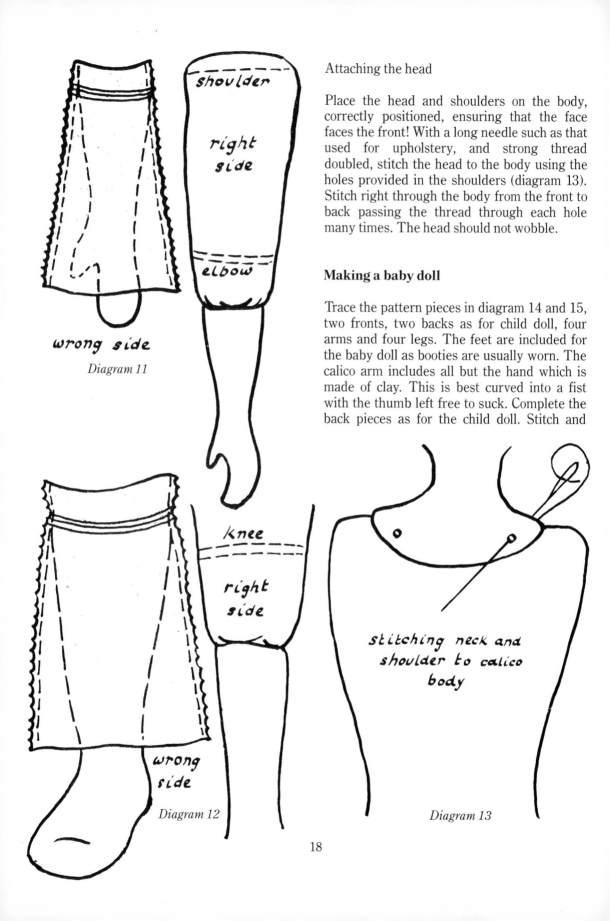

Attaching the head

Place the head and shoulders on the body, correctly positioned, ensuring that the face faces the front! With a long needle such as that used for upholstery, and strong thread doubled, stitch the head to the body using the holes provided in the shoulders (diagram 13). Stitch right through the body from the front to back passing the thread through each hole many times. The head should not wobble.

Making a baby doll

Trace the pattern pieces in diagram 14 and 15, two fronts, two backs as for child doll, four arms and four legs. The feet are included for the baby doll as booties are usually worn. The calico arm includes all but the hand which is made of clay. This is best curved into a fist with the thumb left free to suck. Complete the back pieces as for the child doll. Stitch and

shoulder

right side

elbow

wrong side

Diagram 11

knee

right side

wrong side

Diagram 12

stitching neck and shoulder to calico body

Diagram 13

18

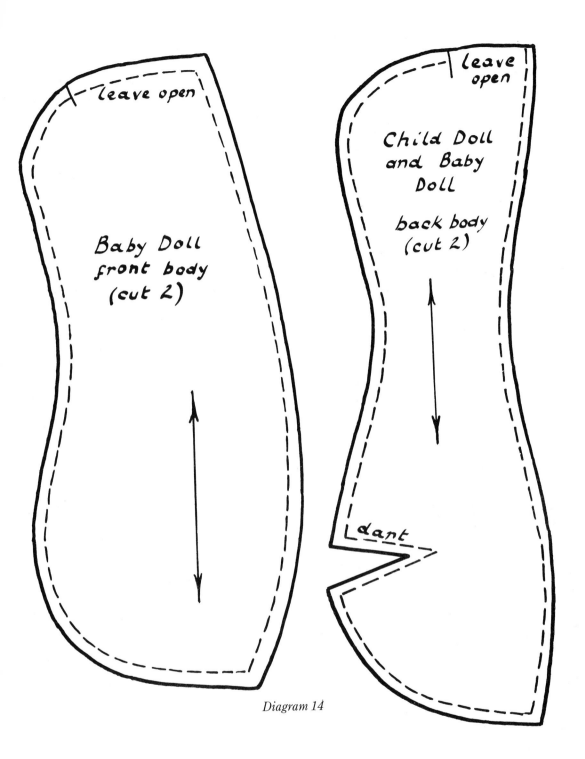

Diagram 14

19

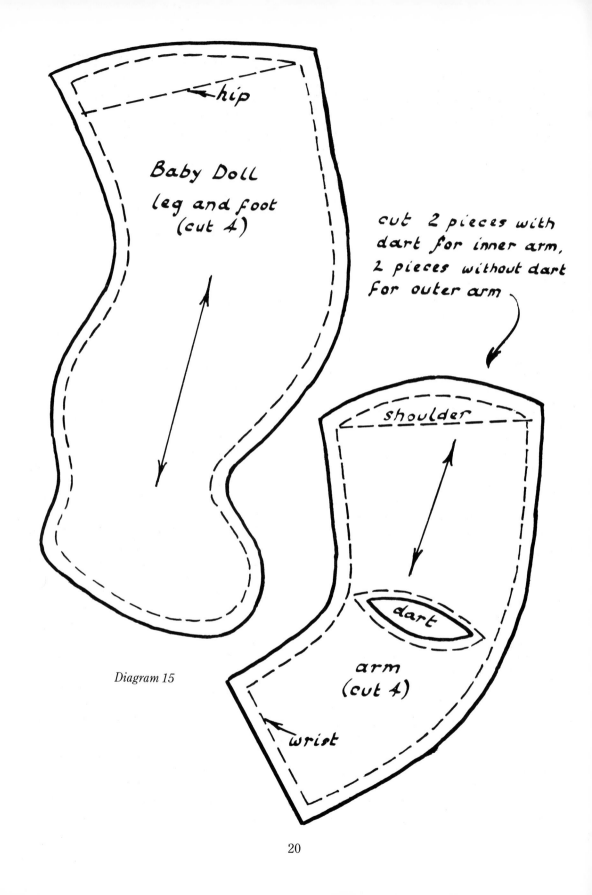

hip

Baby Doll
leg and foot
(cut 4)

cut 2 pieces with
dart for inner arm,
2 pieces without dart
for outer arm

shoulder

dart

arm
(cut 4)

wrist

Diagram 15

20

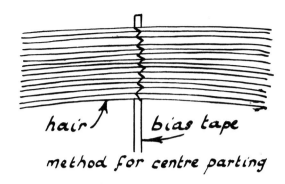

method for centre parting

Diagram 16

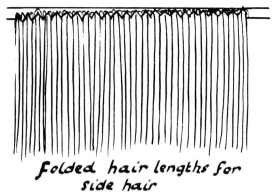

folded hair lengths for side hair

Diagram 17

zig-zag the front seam, place the front and back pieces together, (right sides facing), and stitch and zig-zag. Leave the neck open for stuffing. Close two darts on two front arms only. Place an inner arm next to an undarted outer arm, stitch and zig-zag. Insert the hand as for the arm in the child doll. Stuff the arm until the shoulder is reached, back stitch across the arm at the shoulder. Place the leg pieces in pairs and stitch all round the legs and feet, zig-zag, leave the top open for stuffing. Stuff the legs and stitch across the hip line as indicated. Attach the arms and head as for the child doll. Attach and stitch the legs with care. The knee seam is placed forward, not to the side. Pin the legs in position, the legs should enable the baby doll to sit or crawl. Stitch to the front and back of the doll.

Making a wig

Trace the wig base as in diagram 25. Pin the darts closed and try the base on the doll's head, adjust the darts to make a good fit. Next, decide on the style of hair to suit the doll. Is it to be a curly, wavy, or straight hair-style? Choice of artificial hair depends on the chosen hair-style to some extent. Doll's hair can be purchased in straight nylon lengths or wavy mohair from doll shops or suppliers. Real hair is best of all, but costly. Straight nylon hair is best for plaited styles, although wavy mohair can be used but the strands are more difficult to separate. Mohair is best for waves. Both

types of hair can be curled with heated tongs. Colour choice varies from palest blonde through to black with the addition of a strawberry blonde for red-heads.

There are a number of methods for attaching hair to a wig base. One easy method uses bias binding to match the chosen hair colour, or flesh colour to tone in with the scalp. For a plaited or straight hair-style a centre or side parting is the last step (diagram 16). Cut lengths of hair and place them across the bias strip and zig-zag with matching thread along the strip, spreading hair evenly to conceal bias at the same time. Alternatively the hair can be folded over the bias and zig-zagged in position for lower levels of the wig (diagram 17).

Stitch the darts on the wig base and turn right side out (diagram 18). Following diagram 19, pin hair lengths around the base as shown, leaving a clear area at the centre front unless a fringe is required. Continue to cover the base with layers of hair until the top of the crown is reached, then add a length of bias strip with centre or side parting. If the hair-style suits the doll, stitch the strips in place with running stitches and an occasional back stitch. Alternatively the style shown in diagram 20 may be preferred; two sections of bias strips with hair attached at centre partings are placed one on top of the other and the front hair is then drawn back and tied with a bow to the remainder. Next, place the wig on a wig stand; a plastic skittle makes an excellent stand but if

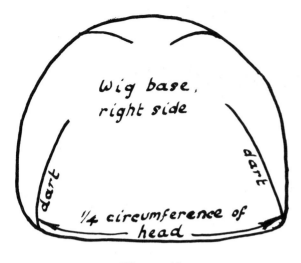

Wig base, right side

dart

dart

¼ circumference of head

Diagram 18

not available, try a padded hair-spray can. Very gently, brush the hair, taking care not to brush the hair out completely from its retaining stitching. Trim the wig with sharp scissors to the desired style and length. Apply UHU glue or fabric adhesive to the inside of the wig base and glue to the doll's scalp. Leave to dry. Check and adjust the hair length. The doll's hair may now be curled and waved with hair tongs with pleasing results. Always curl the hair in towards the head and check the tongs are not too hot or the hair may be singed. Many of the products intended for human hair are equally suitable for arranging dolls' hair. A touch of brilliantine or hair cream will add lustre. Spraying with hair setting spray will hold the style.

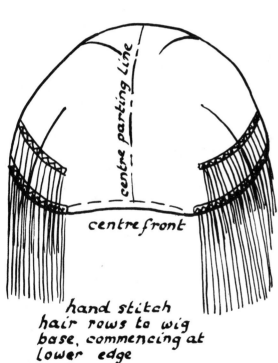

centre parting line

centre front

hand stitch hair rows to wig base, commencing at lower edge

Diagram 19

alternative style using 2 sections with centre parting placed over each other

Diagram 20

22

Child costume dolls

Dressing the Dolls

Fabrics and Equipment

Equipment required:
pinking shears
pins and needles
sewing thread
thimble
embroidery scissors
small buttons
hooks and eyes and pop fasteners
embroidery threads
lace and other trimming
fabric for underwear and costume

Choice of fabric is very important. Natural fibres are preferable—pure wool, cotton lawn, wool/cotton mixtures, etc. Fabric motifs must be of a very small scale, such as the popular 'granny' prints. American fabric designers also specialise in dainty craft fabrics in pure cotton, many of them mix 'n' match types. Sprig floral muslins make charming dresses. Pure silk is very suitable, but costly to buy, small remnants can sometimes be found at lower prices— artificial silks and taffetas are alternatives. Velveteen is the perfect fabric for winter dresses, capes, outer-wear, and suits for boy dolls. Choose the finest cotton lawn available for all underclothing except stiffened under-skirts. Jumble sales sometimes provide excellent fabrics which, when washed and ironed, add a suitably 'antique' look to period dolls. Dress the doll from inside to outside, one layer at a time.

Underwear

Knickers Trace the knicker pattern shown in diagram 24. Pin to a double thickness of fine cotton lawn and cut out the pieces with pinking shears. With running stitch, and an occasional back stitch, stitch the centre front seam and the back seam (diagram 21), but leave open the top of the back seam for the placket opening. Place rows of lace trimming, as indicated on the pattern, to the right sides of the garment and stitch with running stitches. Turn under a narrow hem (diagram 22). On the wrong side, stitch the leg seams from ankle to crotch, through to the other ankle. Cut the waistband to fit the circumference of the doll's waist plus a small overlap of 2-3 cm (¾-1¼ in.), making the band about 4 cm (1¾ in.) wide. Fold in half, stitch one side of the band to the gathered waist edge leaving a small overlap free. Close the open ends and hem the band to the wrong side. Add the button and loop or hook and eye.

Petticoat Trace the pattern pieces shown in diagram 23, front and back bodices. With pinking shears cut around the pinned bodices, two front bodices and four back. Follow the method of making up the bodice as detailed in diagram 26. For the skirt, cut a length of lawn 20 cm (8 in.) deep by 80-100 cm (32½-40 in.) long. Gather the top edge of the skirt and pin to the right side of the bodice, back stitch, turn in the lining of the bodice to enclose the gathers, see diagram 27 for the method. Catch the shoulders together on the wrong side. Turn up and stitch the hem, trim with lace edging or broderie anglaise. Close the back opening with

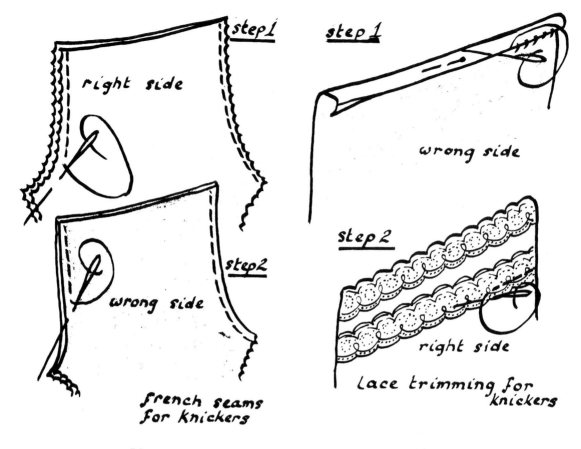

step 1

right side

step 1

wrong side

step 2

wrong side

step 2

right side

french seams
for knickers

lace trimming for
knickers

Diagram 21

Diagram 22

buttons and loops or pop fasteners. Stitch the back seam of the skirt but leave the placket opening free.

Victoria (figure 1)

The dress Use the same pattern pieces as for bodice of the petticoat (diagram 23), then trace the sleeve pattern shown in diagram 25. Victoria's dress is made from sprigged, floral muslin with plain lining to the bodice. Cut one front and two backs in each fabric. Stitch the side and shoulder seams to each set, place the right sides together and stitch across the neck, turn in the back opening, and turn the right side out. Prepare the sleeves; stitch the side seams and gather the sleeve top to fit the

bodice armhole. Check the armhole is sufficiently deep for ease of dressing and adjust as necessary. Pin the sleeve in place, matching dot to shoulder seam and stitch. Narrowly hem the bottom edge of the sleeves, trim with lace and draw up the wrist with shirring elastic as indicated on the pattern. Cut a skirt 20 cm (8 in.) deep by 110 cm (44 in.) and a bottom frill 7 cm (2¾ in.) deep by 220 cm (88 in.)—or two lengths with a centre seam. Gather the skirt to fit the bodice waist and complete as for the petticoat. Gather the frill to fit the bottom of the skirt and stitch, wrong sides together. Turn up a narrow hem and lightly stitch. Trim the neck with gathered lace and add tiny buttons and loops to the back of the bodice.

1   *Victoria, Arthur, Kate and Louise.*

2   *Baby Henrietta and Baby John.*

3 *Edwina.*

4 *Emma.*

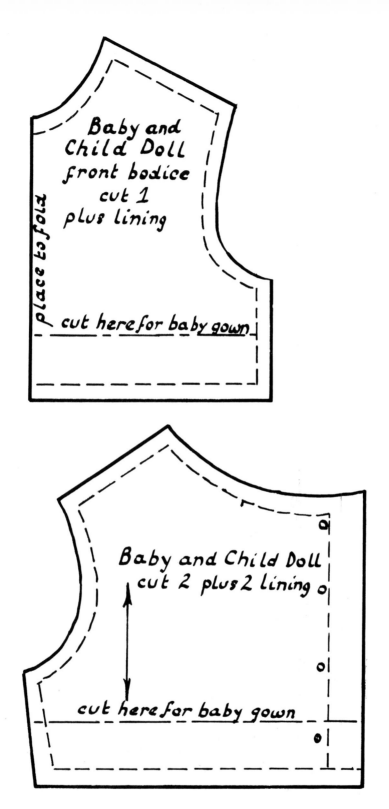

Baby and
Child Doll
front bodice
cut 1
plus lining

place to fold

cut here for baby gown

Baby and Child Doll
cut 2 plus 2 lining

cut here for baby gown

Diagram 23

25

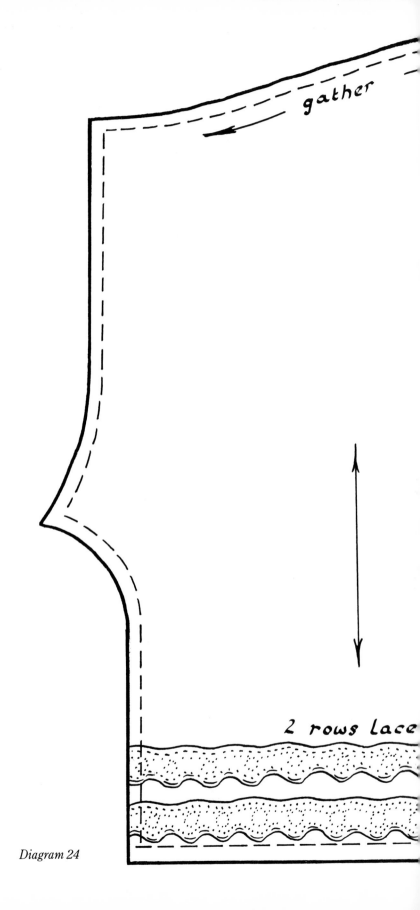

Diagram 24

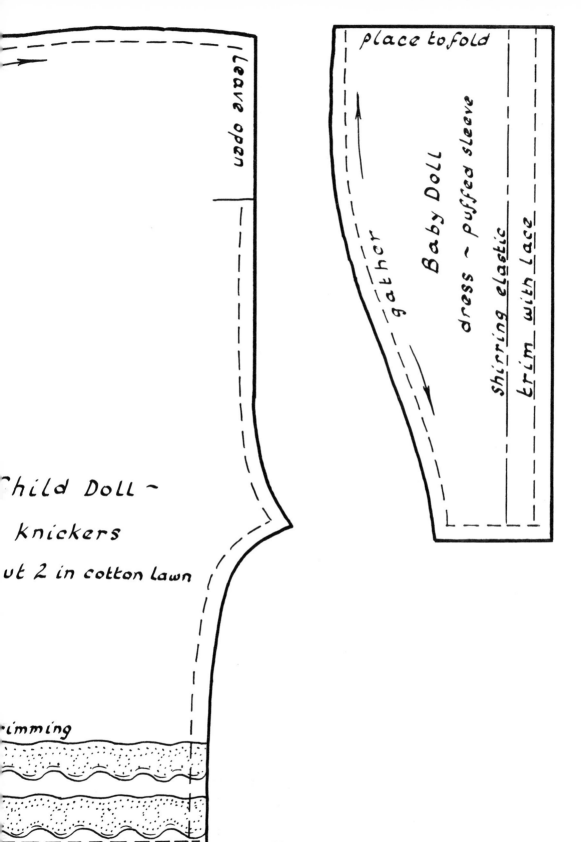

leave open

place to fold

gather

Baby Doll

dress ~ puffed sleeve

shirring elastic

trim with lace

Child Doll ~

knickers

ut 2 in cotton lawn

rimming

27

Diagram 25

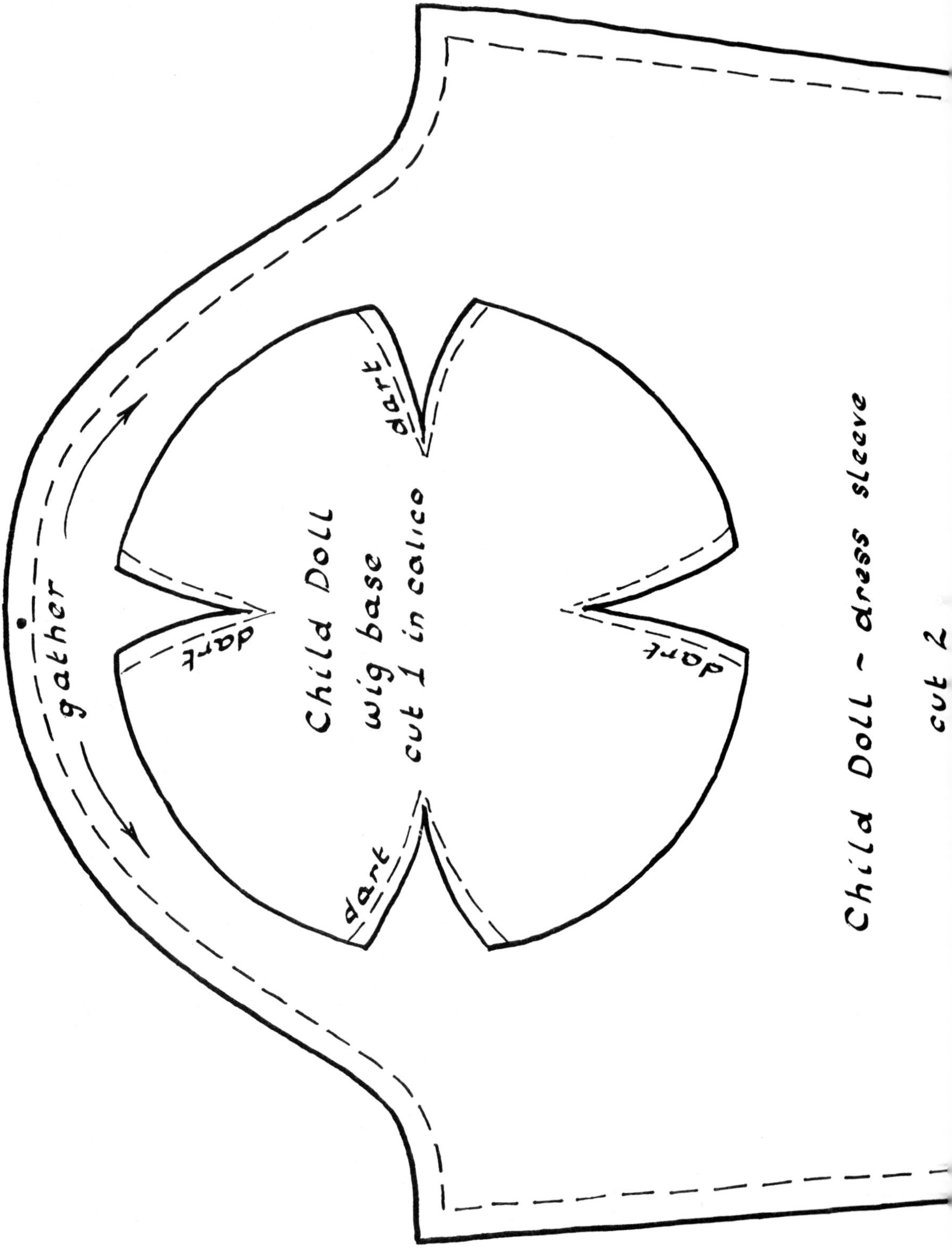

Child Doll
wig base
cut 1 in calico

Child Doll ~ dress sleeve

cut 2

gather

dart

dart

dart

dart

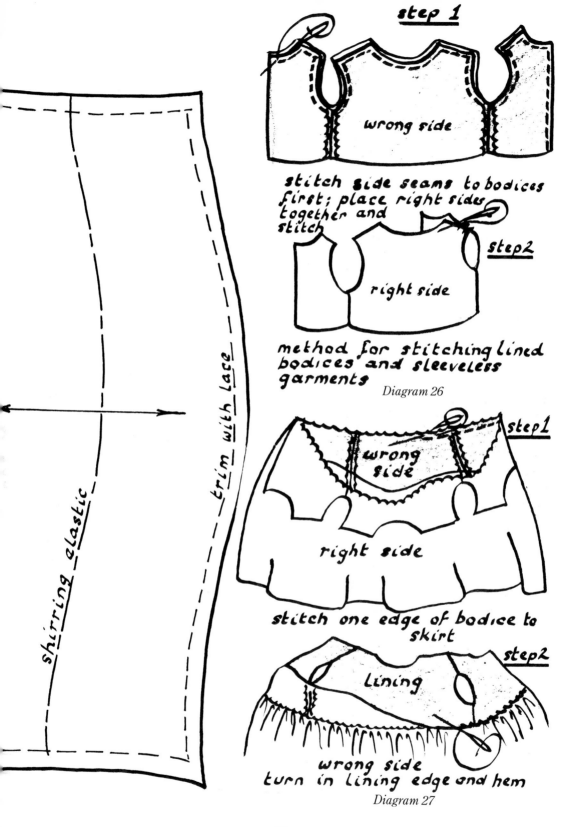

step 1

wrong side

stitch side seams to bodices
first; place right sides
together and
stitch

step 2

right side

method for stitching lined
bodices and sleeveless
garments

Diagram 26

step 1

wrong side

right side

stitch one edge of bodice to
skirt

step 2

Lining

wrong side
turn in lining edge and hem

Diagram 27

trim with lace

shirring elastic

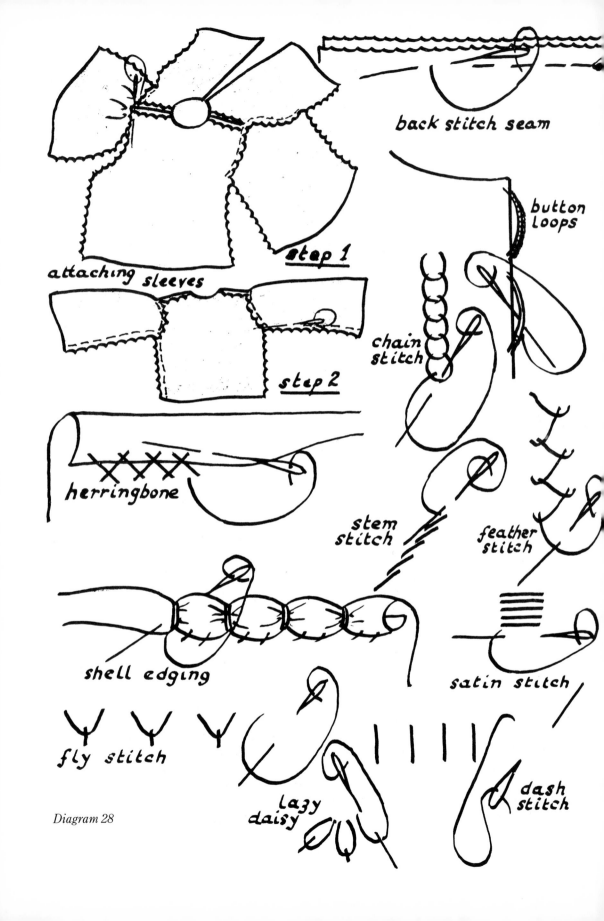

back stitch seam

attaching sleeves

step 1

step 2

button loops

chain stitch

herringbone

stem stitch

feather stitch

shell edging

satin stitch

fly stitch

lazy daisy

dash stitch

Diagram 28

Figure 1 Victoria

The bonnet Victoria's bonnet is made from plaited white craft raffia. Ready-made hats and bonnets are available from doll specialist shops, or the bonnet pattern (diagram 29) may be used, as for Louise.

The boots The boots are made from brown glove leather, for the pattern see diagram 33.

Cut two pieces and stitch the back seam, run a gathering thread around the lower edge and draw up to fit a doll's foot. Cut two inner and two outer soles from stiff cardboard or art board. Place the inner sole next to the doll's foot, put the boot on the doll and with clear adhesive, glue the gathered edge of the boot over the sole. Apply more adhesive to the sole

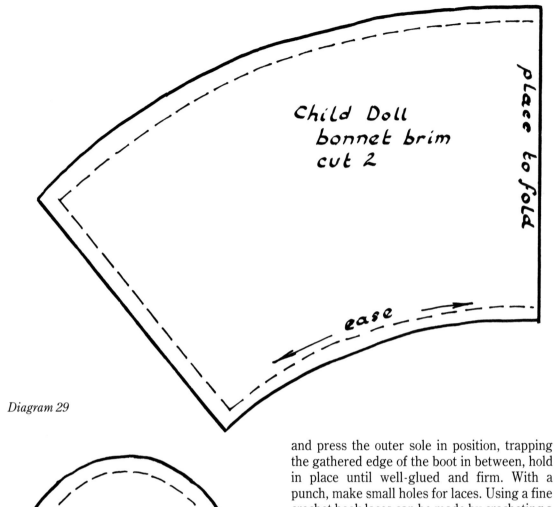

place to fold

Child Doll
bonnet brim
cut 2

ease

Diagram 29

bonnet
back

cut 1 plus lining

and press the outer sole in position, trapping the gathered edge of the boot in between, hold in place until well-glued and firm. With a punch, make small holes for laces. Using a fine crochet hook laces can be made by crocheting a chain of brown thread to the required length.

Kate and Louise (figure 2)

The dresses Kate and Louise's dresses require a little more dressmaking skill. Using the patterns in diagram 30 and 31 for the bodice and sleeve, and the patterns in diagram 32 and 33 for the skirt, trace all the pattern pieces required. Louise's dress is made of a cotton granny print and Kate's from another sprigged muslin lined in plain cotton. With pinking shears, cut two sleeves; one front yoke and two back yokes plus the same in lining. Join the two skirt pattern pieces together and cut one skirt, noting the length to be extended. Cut four

Figure 2 Kate and Louise

collars (diagram 30). Join the shoulder seams of the bodice and lining. Leave the lining on one side for now. Gather the top of the skirt to fit the yoke, pin in place matching under-arm recess on the skirt to the shoulders. Leave the top shoulder on the yoke free. Stitch the yoke to skirt, leaving the armholes free. Stitch the side seam of the sleeve and gather the top to fit the armhole. Insert the sleeve, pin in place, and stitch. Join the two pairs of collars together, turn right side out, press, and attach to the neck opening. Pin the lining to the yoke, right sides together; stitch across the neck enclosing the collars, stitch down the back openings. On the wrong side fold in the lower edge of the bodice lining and hem. Close the back seam of

the skirt, leaving a placket opening free. Turn up sleeve and skirt hems and stitch. Trim both with decorative doll trimming. Run a length of shirring elastic at the wrist to fit. Trim the centre collar with a velvet bow.

Bonnet Louise's bonnet is made of cream satin with toning lining. Trace the pattern pieces shown in diagram 29. Cut two bonnet backs and two bonnet brims and one brim in Vilene. Make up the bonnet and lining as two separate pieces, easing in the bonnet back brim to fit the horseshoe-shaped back bonnet. With right sides together stitch the two brim edges together. Turn right side out and narrowly turn in the raw edges and hem together. Trim with

33

lace and rosettes and add ribbon at the chin. Kate's straw hat is made from craft raffia, plaited and sewn in a floppy style.

Shoes Kate and Louise have shoes made from the pattern in diagram 34, in brown or gold glove leather. Stitch the front and back seams as shown, turn right side out and complete as for Victoria's boots. Punch a hole in the strap and add a bead opposite to act as a button.

Stockings All three dolls have stockings made from white finger bandage. Pull the bandage up to the hips, cut off any surplus just beyond the tip of the toe and gather the ends together, fasten off.

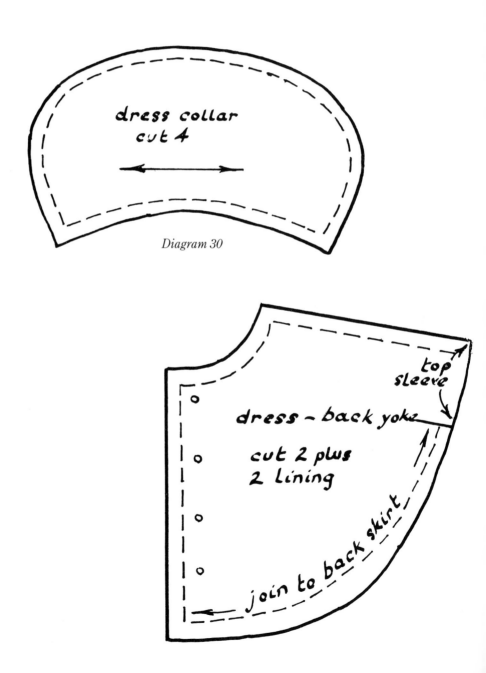

dress collar
cut 4

Diagram 30

top sleeve

dress – back yoke

cut 2 plus 2 lining

join to back skirt

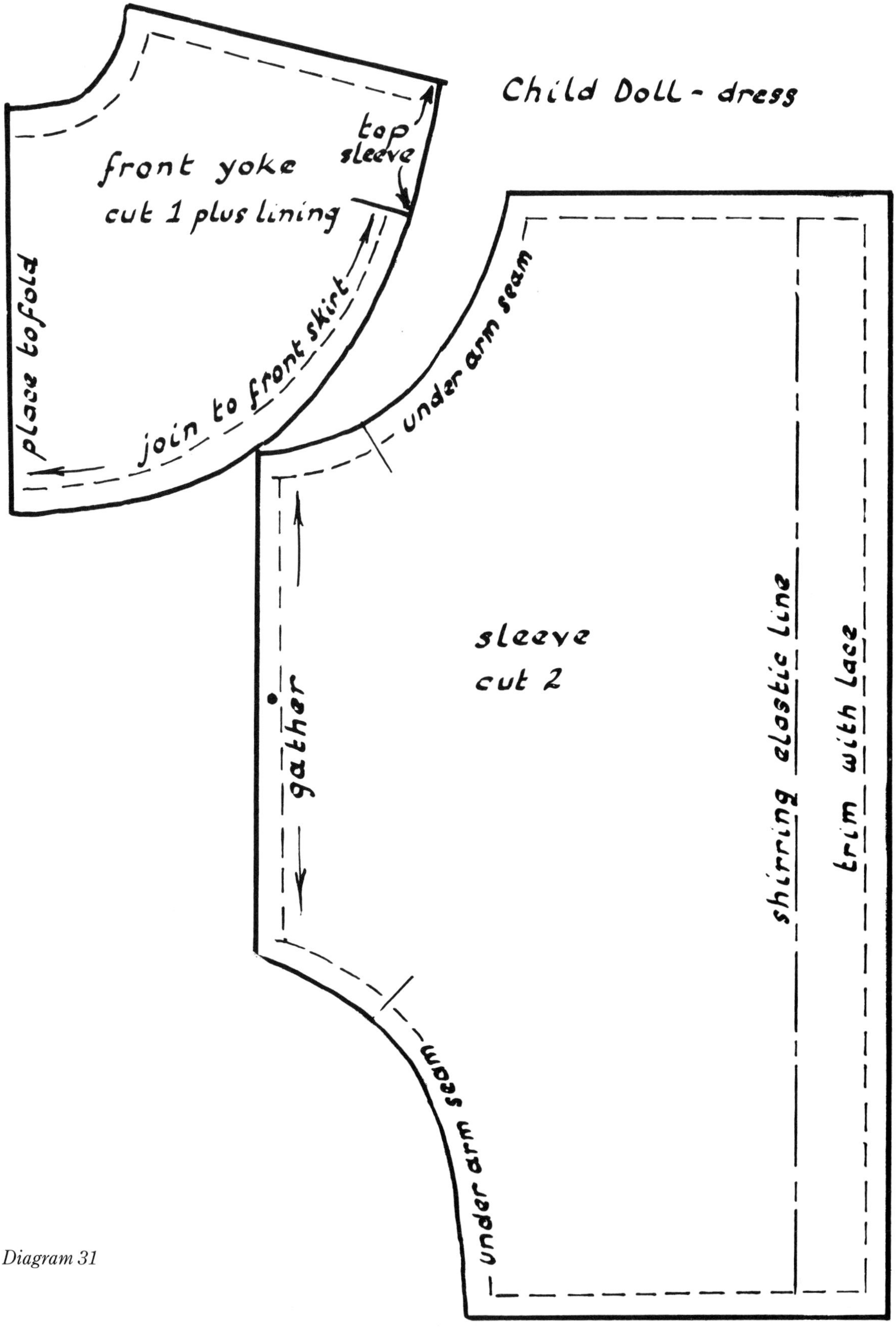

Child Doll - dress

front yoke
cut 1 plus lining

place to fold

top sleeve

join to front skirt

under arm seam

sleeve
cut 2

gather

shirring elastic line

trim with lace

under arm seam

Diagram 31

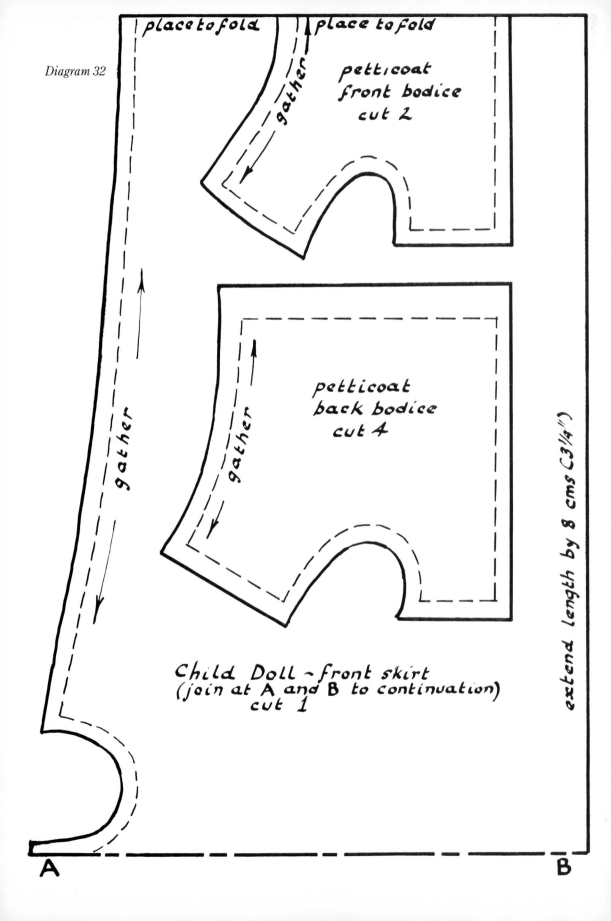

Diagram 32

place to fold   place to fold

petticoat
front bodice
cut 2

gather

petticoat
back bodice
cut 4

gather

gather

Child Doll ~ front skirt
(join at A and B to continuation)
cut 1

extend length by 8 cms (3¼")

A   B

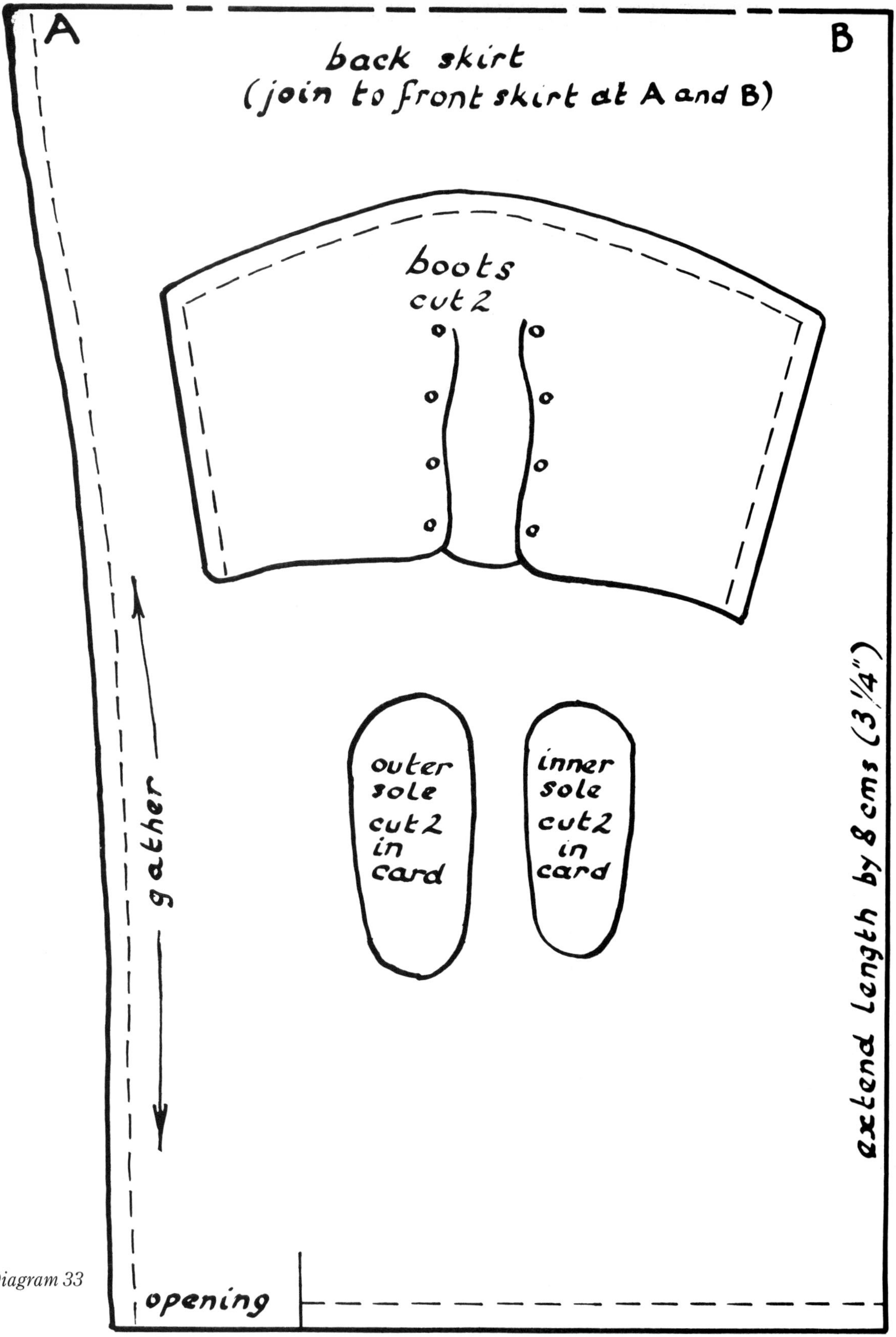

A   B

back skirt
(join to front skirt at A and B)

boots
cut 2

outer
sole
cut 2
in
card

inner
sole
cut 2
in
card

gather

extend length by 8 cms (3¼")

Diagram 33

opening

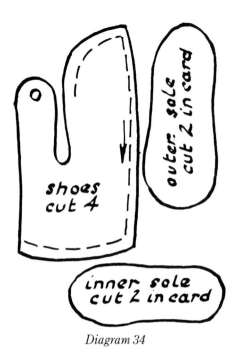

shoes
cut 4

outer sole
cut 2 in card

inner sole
cut 2 in card

Diagram 34

Figure 3 Baby Henrietta

Baby Henrietta (figure 3)

Dress Henrietta's christening gown is made from pure silk chiffon over a satin underskirt and bodice. A cream wool/cotton petticoat is also worn beneath the gown. The pattern pieces for the gown are as for Victoria with slightly shortened bodice, as indicated on the pattern, and the length of the skirt increased to allow for rows of tucking as for a full length Victorian baby gown.

Bonnet The bonnet is ruched and gathered pure silk trimmed with ecru lace, and covers Henrietta's clay curls which are painted pale blonde.

Make up all the garments as for Victoria with a chosen number of tucks worked.

Baby John (figure 4)

Wig Baby John has a wig suitable for a toddler doll. It is made from good quality silky, long-haired, blonde fur-fabric which looks convincing when made up. Make a pattern from the child doll's wig (diagram 25) but cut it into four equal segments. Pin the pattern pieces to the fur-fabric in such a manner that the fur lies straight from the centre crown point to the centre of a segment at face edge. Cut the fabric on the wrong side with sharp scissors, ensuring that the backing only is cut and not the fur-pile. Pin the pieces together and try the hair cap on the head of the doll. It may be necessary to increase the curve of the segments to fit the head more closely. When a correct fit is achieved, stitch close to the edge with firm stitches. Turn right side out and tease out any trapped lengths of hair with a pin. If correctly sewn, no seams should be apparent. Glue hair to the scalp with clear adhesive. Trim

Figure 4 Baby John

the hair to a chosen style with a fringe at the front.

Cross-over vest Using 3-ply baby wool and 2¼ mm (No. 13) needles, cast on 36 stitches (sts) for the back. Knit (k) 1, purl (p) 1 for four rows. Change to size 2¾ mm (No. 12) needles and stocking stitch (st st) for 22 rows. Next four rows: cast on 3 sts at beg. of each row for sleeve. Following four rows: cast on 8 sts at beg. of each row. St st for 20 rows on 80 sts. *Neck shaping:* k 30, cast off 20 sts, continue on rem. 30 sts for left front. St st for 13 rows but at the neck edge, cast on 1 st on every row.

Next row: at sleeve edge cast off 8 sts at beg. of row, and following alt. row. Then 3 sts twice at beg. of next two alt. rows, at the same time cont. to inc. 1 st at neck edge on every row. Keeping armhole edge straight, cont. to inc. at neck edge on every row until 34 sts on needle. Cont. straight without further shaping until front matches back in length, when arm folded over and incs and decs matched up, to commencement of ribbing. Change to 2¼ mm needles and k1, p1 for four rows. Cast off loosely. Complete right front as for left front, reversing all shapings. *Sleeves:* using 2¼ mm needles, pick up 32 sts at sleeve ends and k1, p1 for five rows for wrist. Cast off in rib. Sew up side and sleeve seams. With a fine crochet hook pick up a st from each row up both fronts of the vest and across the back neck. Crochet three rows in double crochet, making two buttonhole loops on the last row at the waist. Sew on two small buttons to match button loops at the side of the vest. Alternatively, knit a garter stitch border.

Pilch Using 3-ply wool and 2¼ mm (No. 13) needles, cast on 36 sts. K1, p1 rib for three rows. Eyelet row for elastic—k1, (wool forward, k2 tog.) to last 2 sts, k2. K1, p1 rib for three rows. Inc. row: k1, (k twice into next st, k7) to last 2 sts, k2 (41 sts). Change to 2¾ mm (size 12) needles and garter stitch (every row knit). *Shape for back:* k26 turn; k10 turn; k15 turn; k20 turn; k25 turn; k30 turn; k to end of row. Next row: inc. at both ends of row (43 sts). K10 rows. Inc. at both ends of row. K10 rows. Inc. at both ends of row (47 sts). K10 rows. Cast off 8 sts at beg. of next two rows (31 sts). Cast off 2 sts at beg. of each following row until 9 sts rem. K6 rows. Cast on 2 sts at beg. of following row until 31 sts. Cast on 8 sts at beg. of next 2 rows (47 sts). K10 rows. Next row: Dec at both ends of row. Rep. these 11 rows until 41 sts rem. and front measures the same as back to commencement of ribbing. Dec row: k1 (k2 tog., k7) to end of row, k2 (36 sts). Change to 2¼ mm needles, k1, p1 rib for three rows. Make eyelet row as before, k1, p1 rib for three rows, cast off in rib loosely. With 2¼ mm needles pick up 54 sts at row ends of leg shaping. K1, p1 rib for six rows. Cast off loosely in rib. Repeat for other leg. Sew up side seams and run a length of fine elastic through eyelet holes.

Romper top John's romper top is made of white wool/cotton mixture. The bodice and sleeve are as for baby Henrietta. The skirt of the romper is a continuous length of fabric 14 cm (5¾ in.) deep. The length measurement depends on the choice of smocked or gathered skirt.

Smocked skirt For a smocked skirt triple the chest measurement; a ½ cm (¼ in.) dot transfer was used to a depth of 4 cm (1¾ in.). Embroidery books in libraries advise on smocking stitches. Alternatively several rows of gathering will suffice. The sleeves and neck are trimmed with lace. The sleeve is gathered at the wrist with shirring elastic.

Bonnet John's bonnet is made from matching wool/cotton fabric trimmed with immitation 'swan's down' feather trimming, obtainable by the metre at good haberdashers.

Arthur (figure 5)

Arthur is dressed in a velveteen suit and hat, and a silk blouse. His *underwear* is of a simpler style than his sister's but the same pattern pieces are used. His *long pants* are made of cotton lawn, using the knicker pattern in diagram 24 but omitting the rows of lace and substituting a narrow hem threaded with elastic. The gathered edge should reach just below knee and the length should be shortened accordingly. Stitch up the back seam, ignoring the back opening; instead, a front opening is left. Add a narrow waistband.

Liberty bodice In place of a petticoat, Arthur wears a liberty bodice made from a wool/cotton mixture. Use the pattern in diagram 23 for the bodice but increase the length to reach the hip. Make the bodice of double fabric, cutting four backs and two fronts (see diagram 26). Close

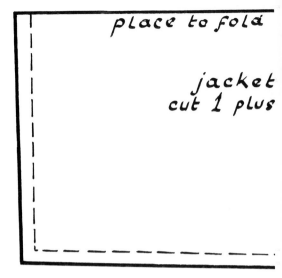

Boy Doll – suit in velveteen

Figure 5 Arthur

40

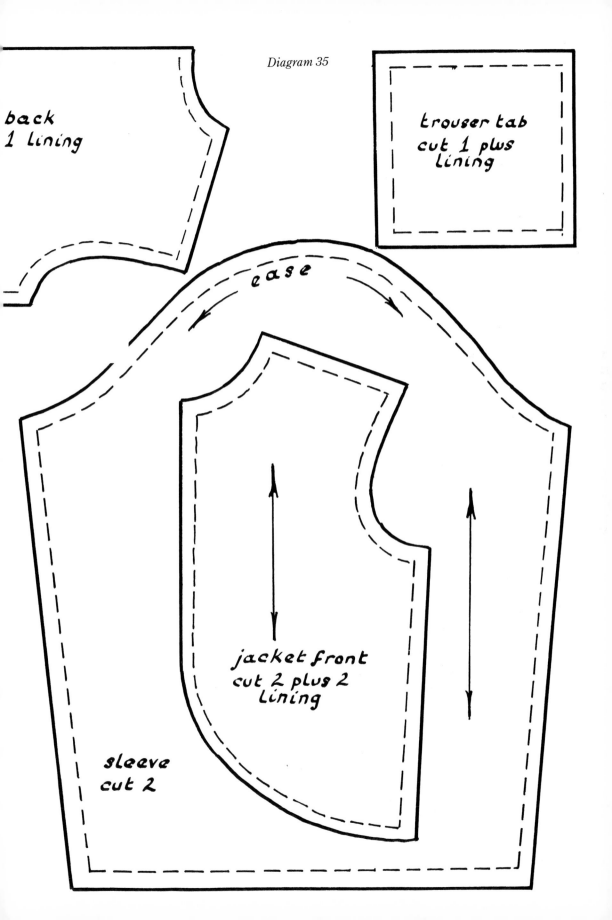

Diagram 35

back
1 lining

trouser tab
cut 1 plus
lining

ease

jacket front
cut 2 plus 2
lining

sleeve
cut 2

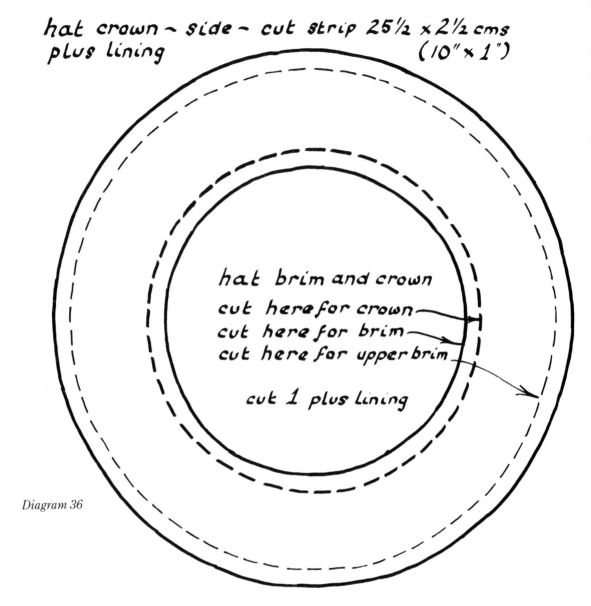

hat crown - side - cut strip 25½ x 2½ cms
plus lining   (10" x 1")

hat brim and crown
cut here for crown
cut here for brim
cut here for upper brim

cut 1 plus lining

Diagram 36

the back opening with buttons and loops. To make the liberty bodice authentic, stitch on bands of narrow white ribbon from the shoulder seam to the lower edge, four to the front and two each side of backs, giving the garments additional strength and support.

Blouse Arthur's blouse is made of pure or imitation silk in ecru. The bodice pattern on diagram 23 is again used, with added length and some extra seam allowance to fit over the wool/cotton bodice. The sleeve pattern is as shown in diagram 25, as for the girls, complete in the same way (diagram 28). Stitch a ruched length of lace down centre front. Make a Peter Pan collar from diagram 30 and complete as for Louise. A row of gathered lace is stitched all round each collar edge. Close the blouse with buttons and loops or pop fasteners. Hem the lower edge and run the narrow elastic through the hem.

Suit Arthur's suit is made of velveteen and the jacket and hat are lined with a matching acetate lining fabric. Commence with the trousers of single fabric using the knicker pattern on diagram 22. Again, adjust the leg length to a narrow hem just below the knee and make a centre front opening. Add the waistband and fasten with a hook and eye. The front opening is concealed behind a fly tab (diagram 35); stitch two sections together on all three sides, turn right side out and pin to the trousers by the raw edges. Turn the raw edges under and hem in position. Stitch the leg seams and insert narrow elastic. The jacket pattern is found on diagram 35 and is lined except for the sleeves. Stitch the fronts to the back, repeat for the lining, place the right sides together and stitch all round, leaving the neck edge free to turn right side out. Close the neck invisibly, concealing the raw edges. Join the side seams of the sleeves and gather the top of the sleeve, insert the sleeve ensuring that the jacket will pass easily over the blouse; if it is too tight increase the depth of the armhole. Trim the jacket with narrow braid edging and fasten with a hook and eye. Conceal the hook with a satin bow.

Hat The hat pattern is shown in diagram 36. Stitch the end seams of crown sides, pin to the round crown, stretching slightly to fit, stitch. Repeat with the lining. Place the lining in the crown concealing all raw edges. Cut two brims in velveteen, one slightly smaller than the other, the upper brim being the smaller of the two, this will help to curve the brim in a slight sailor style. Stitch the outer edges of the brim together, stretching the smaller to match the larger; pin and stitch to the crown, tuck in the acetate lining over the join and hem. Decorate the crown with narrow braid and feathers. A length of cord elastic may be added to the hat to hold it in place, concealing the elastic at the back of the head.

Socks Socks can be made either of finger bandage or from the ribbed welts of discarded, machine-knit sweaters of appropriate colours. Cut straight tubes or ribbing and oversew at the back of the sock.

Shoes Shoes are made of glove or patent leather in black (diagram 34). The front of the shoes may be decorated with satin bows or a buckle.

Adult costume dolls

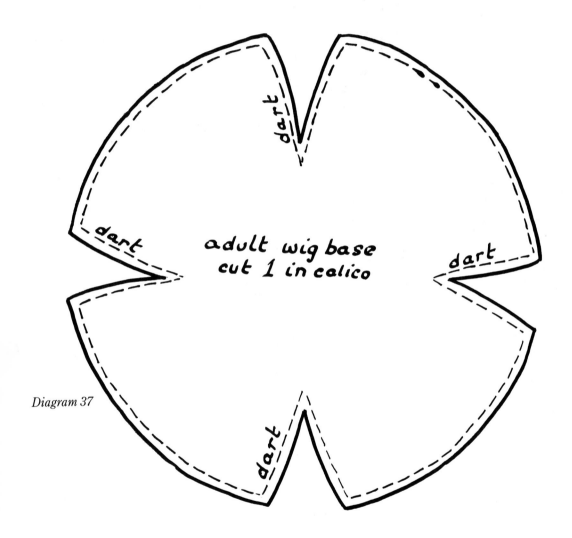

Diagram 37

Adult Costume Dolls

Adult dolls are made in much the same way as child dolls but with different body patterns, as appropriate to sex. For instructions on how to make a head refer to chapter one but with the following modifications: the size of the polystyrene ball should be 6 or 7 cm (2¼-2¾ in.). A 6 cm (2¼ in.) ball is used for a woman doll and a 7 cm (2¾ in.) for a male. As the bodies of adult dolls are wider than that of a child doll the stand needs a wider shoulder support.

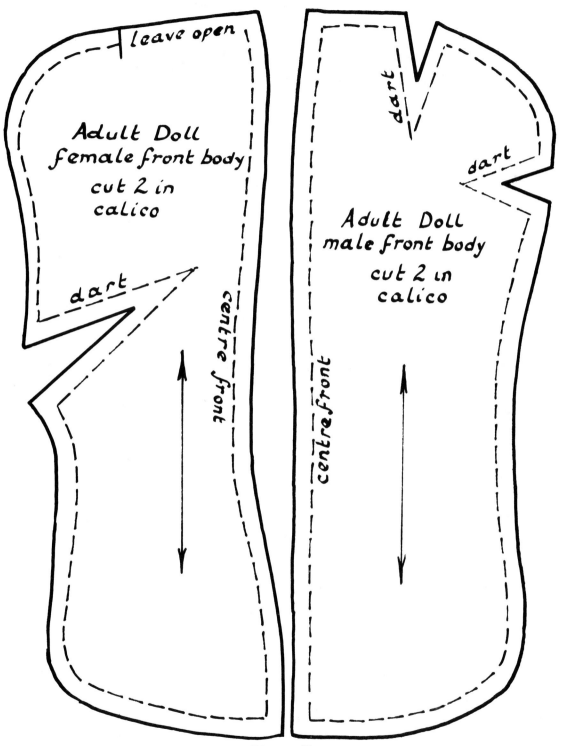

leave open

Adult Doll
female front body
cut 2 in
calico

dart

centre front

Adult Doll
male front body
cut 2 in
calico

dart

dart

centre front

Diagram 38

45

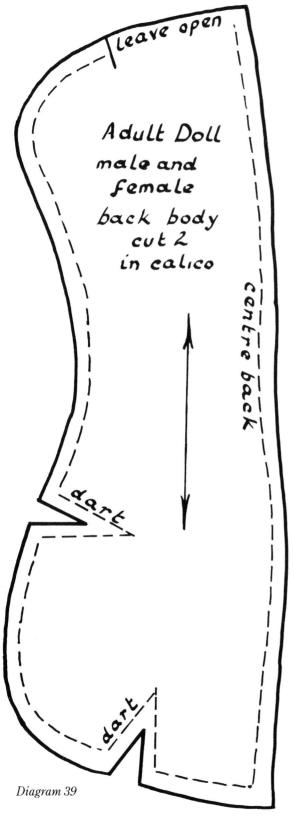

Adult Doll
male and
female
back body
cut 2
in calico

leave open

centre back

dart

dart

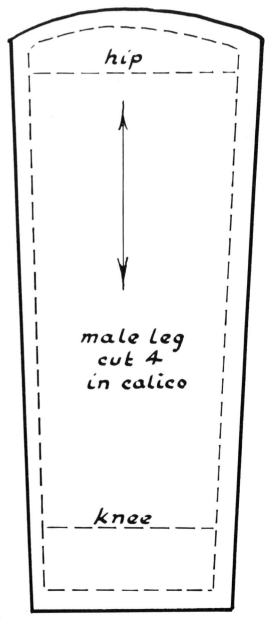

hip

male leg
cut 4
in calico

knee

Existing stands can be temporarily amended by using self-drying clay as a filler (diagram 2). Leave the padding to dry before resting the new shoulder shapes on the shoulder dowel. Set up the adjusted stand as for previous dolls but with an increased distance left below the ball for the neck. Make the wigs in the same way as before but using the pattern in diagram 37. The head shape and face must also be altered to resemble an adult rather than a child. Again, a book on drawing portraits or

Diagram 39

Diagram 40

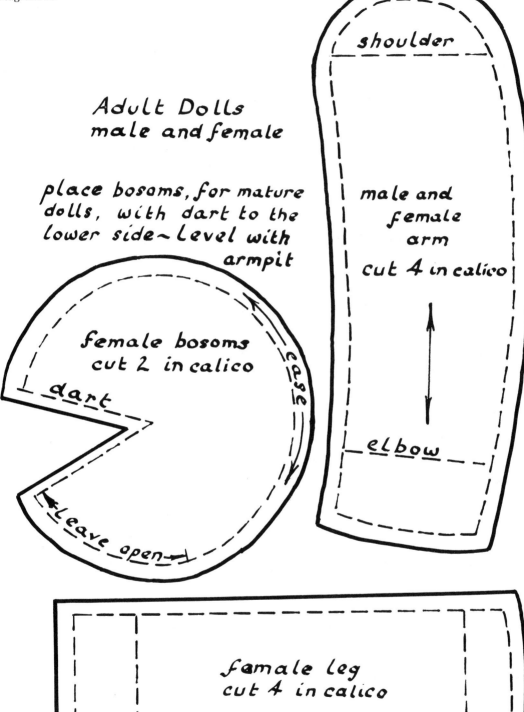

Adult Dolls
male and female

place bosoms, for mature
dolls, with dart to the
lower side ~ level with
armpit

female bosoms
cut 2 in calico

dart

ease

← leave open →

shoulder

male and
female
arm

cut 4 in calico

elbow

female leg
cut 4 in calico

knee

hip

anatomy will assist, also photographs if they are large enough. Commence with a female head before attempting a male head. Observe the components which make up a beautiful face and try to emulate the same clear, clean-cut lines to the face, the straight nose, the graceful chin, wide eyes, etc. The guide lines for the features will be the same as for child dolls but the outlines of the jaw and cheeks should be less rounded. The eyebrows should be a little more arched, the lips have a clear bow and the chin sharper. Complete a head using the same method as described for child dolls; sand and paint the face but note that some of the shading will be a little deeper in colour.

Paper patterns for calico bodies are shown in diagrams 38 and 39. Trace the pattern pieces, pin to the calico and cut the pieces as directed. Close the darts to the front and back pieces, stitch the centre seams and zig-zag for strength. Cut four leg pieces and stitch two sets together, zig-zagging as before. Cut four arm pieces and four leg pieces and stitch two sets of each together (diagram 40). Stitch the front and back bodies together and the right sides together, leaving the neck edge open for stuffing.

Make the arms and legs from self-drying clay or Fimo clay. The latter is strongly recommended for adult dolls as this type of clay lends itself to slim wrists and ankles and human-looking hands with delicate fingers that can be manipulated to mimic almost any human hand function such as holding a basket of flowers or a parasol (diagram 41). Use rose nail polish on the tips of fingers. Complete the arms and legs using the same method as for the child dolls but stitch the arms to the shoulders in a continuous curve and the lower edge of the arm to form the underarm. Similarly with the legs, front edges to the front hips, rear edges to the seat, checking that adequate movement is retained and the doll can sit easily.

With strong thread join the head to the body as before, ensuring the angle of the larger head is correct.

The patterns given for the female dolls have the figure of a young woman, suitable for a debutante's 'coming-out' gown or a bridal gown. If a more mature figure is required add separate bosoms (diagram 40). Close and stitch the dart; pin the bosom in the correct position with the end of the dart on a level with the arm-pit. Turn in the raw edges, shaping the bosom to the centre as you do so, leaving space for stuffing along one edge. A good figure depends on placing the bosom correctly, attaching it well, and filling it evenly.

A male doll is created in much the same manner but a more manly body pattern is used (diagram 38), incorporating broader shoulders, slimmer hips, and a stronger pair of legs (diagram 40). Other than differences in the body, male features have to be achieved. Again, a good drawing or photograph will help. The chin will need to be more rugged, the brow broader, the neck thicker, etc. A moustache or beard can help to emphasise masculinity. Tiny pieces of fur fabric glued to the completed face with clear adhesive look very authentic. They can be trimmed with sharp scissors and brilliantined for sheen. The shape of the moustache can be given uplift or a twirl with a mixture of sugar and water to hold the style.

Dressing the Dolls

First, it is necessary to decide on the theme of the collection. Is it to be a collection of dolls from around the world or a period costume family? The patterns commencing with diagram 43 cover almost all requirements for period costume dolls and those beginning at diagram 58 for folk costume dolls. But the two types of pattern pieces often intermingle and the underclothing is common to both.

If the dolls are to be folk costume dolls a book entitled *Folk Costumes of the World* in the Blandford colour series will be immensely helpful. Alternatively make your own sketches whilst abroad (diagram 42). As I had no paints or crayons available, I made notes on a rough sketch indicating colours, and choice of embroidery stitches. It is often the colour scheme in a folk costume that marks it out from

5   *Arabella and Harold.*

6   *Jan, Aniela, Halina, Stefan and Zofia.*

7   *Pierre, Said, Dolores,*
Geronimo and Marie.

8   *Madame Butterfly.*

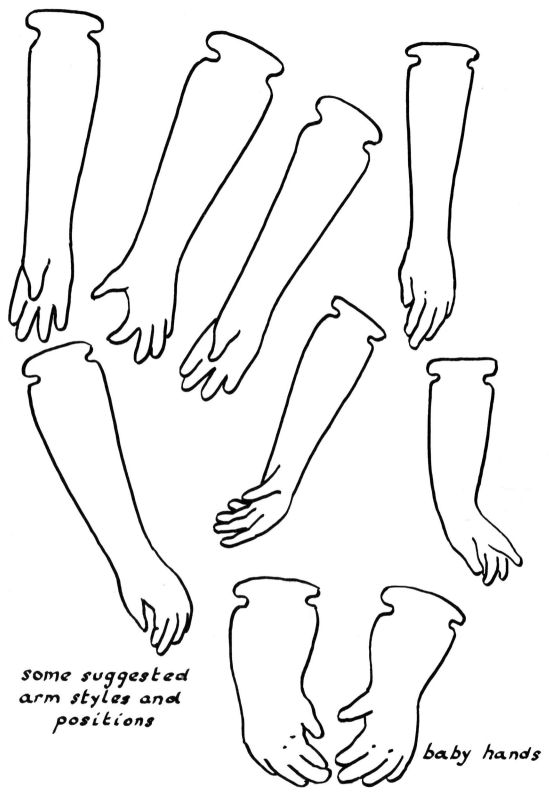

some suggested
arm styles and
positions

baby hands

Diagram 41

49

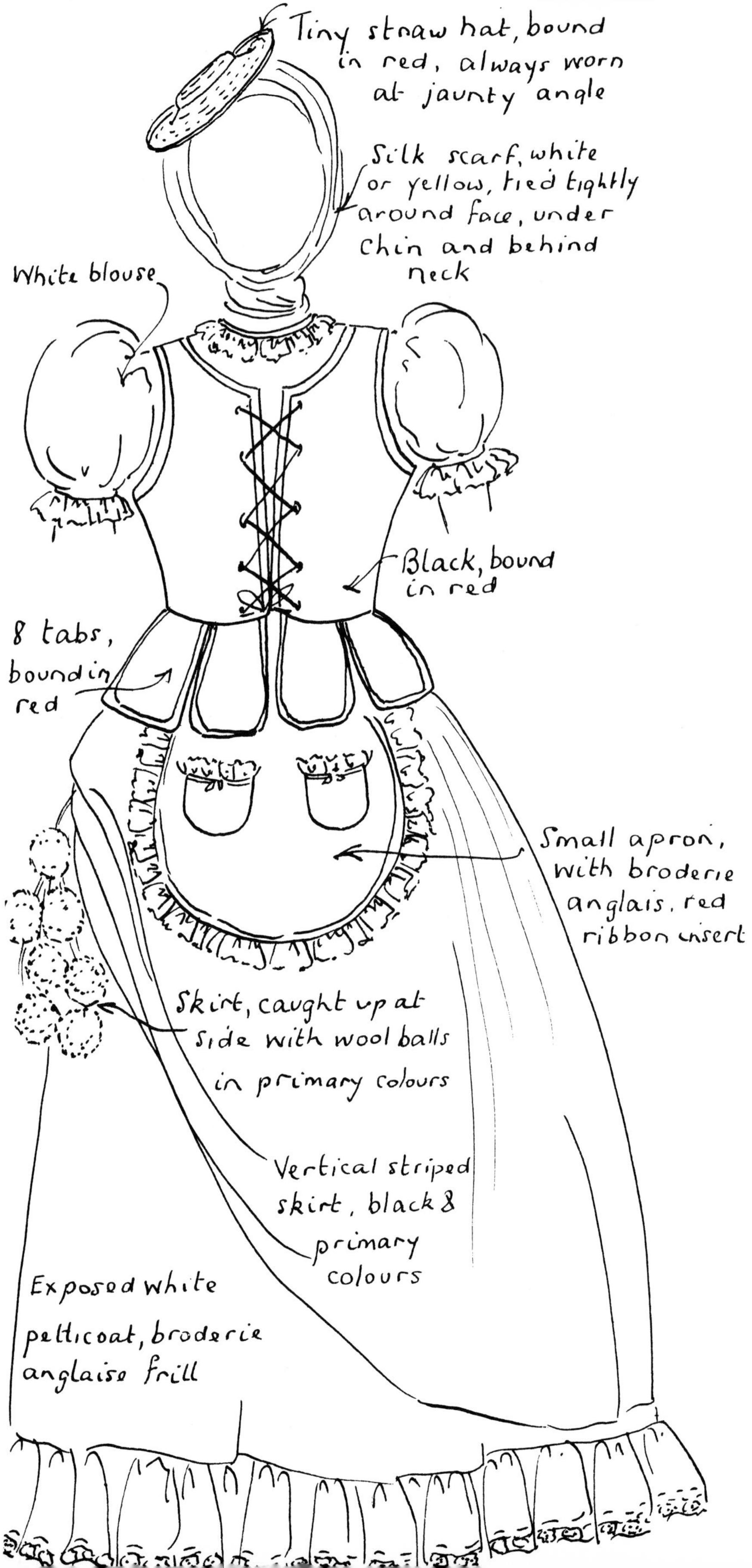

Tiny straw hat, bound in red, always worn at jaunty angle

Silk scarf, white or yellow, tied tightly around face, under chin and behind neck

White blouse

Black, bound in red

8 tabs, bound in red

Small apron, with broderie anglais, red ribbon insert

Skirt, caught up at side with wool balls in primary colours

Vertical striped skirt, black & primary colours

Exposed white petticoat, broderie anglaise frill

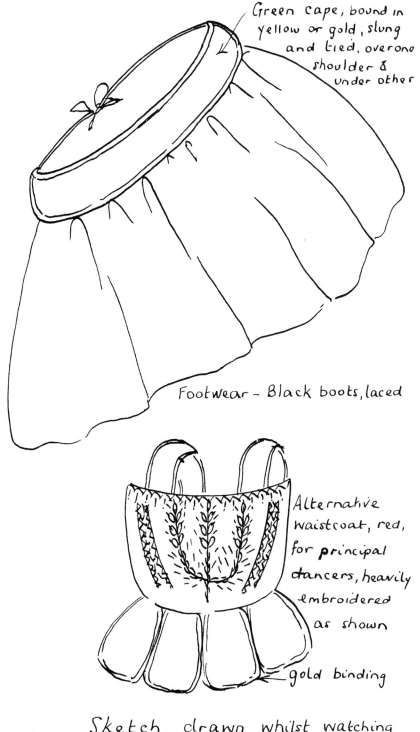

Green cape, bound in yellow or gold, slung and tied, over one shoulder & under other

Footwear - Black boots, laced

Alternative waistcoat, red, for principal dancers, heavily embroidered as shown

gold binding

<u>Sketch</u>, drawn whilst watching Canary Island dancers; costume verified in repose and inked in later.

Diagram 42

other countries with similar styles of dress.

Harold (figure 6)

Underwear The paper pattern for trousers and pants is shown in diagram 43. Using pinking shears and a fine cotton lawn fabric, cut two pieces for the pants using the guide line indicated, include fly extensions, one for the right fly and one for the left. Also cut a shaped waistband. Stitch the back seams and the front seam as far as the fly opening. Turn in and hem the fly extensions and overlap the left fly over the right. Stitch the leg seams. Hem the lower leg edge of the pants. Stitch the facing to the right side, turn to the wrong side and hem. Attach a pop fastener to the fly.

Shirt Trace the patterns for the shirt (diagrams 44 and 45); cut one shirt back, two fronts, two sleeves and cuffs. The detached collar is shown in diagram 45. Make up the shirt as in diagram 28, using white cotton lawn and a satin type of fabric for the detached collar. Leave the bottom of the sleeves open for about 1½ cm (¾ in.), gather to fit the cuff and stitch the cuff to the right side of the sleeve, hem to the wrong side. Fold the front facings over and hem, hem the lower edge of the shirt. Face the neck edge with bias strip. Sew tiny pearl buttons to the front of the shirt and cuffs with matching buttonholes. Make up the collar from the chosen fabric, cutting two pieces plus one of Vilene. Stitch around the two upper edges of the collar plus the Vilene, turn to the right side, trim the Vilene and press. Turn in the lower edges of the collar and catch together narrowly. Fasten the collar to the shirt with small pop fasteners to act as front and back studs. Make a bow tie from taffeta or satin ribbon.

Trousers Use the pattern in diagram 43 but cut on the line marked *Krakowiak*, also cut a trouser facing. Reduce the length by about 3-5 cm (1¼-2 in.) and make up as for the pants. The choice of fabric is a light wool or wool/cotton mixture, with a small fleck or check pattern. Endeavour to choose a check as

Figure 6 Harold

small as possible or Harold will look a 'flashy' dresser. Use herringbone stitch to hem the fly. Adjust the leg length to fit below the knee, leave a 2 cm (¾ in.) seam free at the knee for the placket opening; make a pleat to the outside of each leg and face the leg ends with acetate bias strip. Invisibly hem to the wrong side and close the plackets with small pop fastener.

Waistcoat This is made from a contrasting fabric, wool/cotton mixtures, velveteen or brocade. Use the pattern pieces given in diagram 63, altering the angled lower front edge to a curving slope. Cut one back and two fronts and the same in lining fabric. Make up as diagram 26, turn the right side out and fold in the raw edges narrowly and close invisibly with neat oversewing. Trim with doll's braid. Use three or four tiny pearl buttons and matching loops to close.

Golf stockings These may be knitted, or can be made from strips of ribbed welts from a discarded fine woollen sweater. To knit the socks use a small ball of 4-ply beige wool and a few scraps of contrast wool in green, yellow and burgundy or brown plus a pair of size 0 (No. 13) knitting needles. Using beige wool loosely cast on 30 sts. K1, p1 for two rows. Join in the green yarn for mock Fair Isle pattern; *3rd row* k1 beige, k1 green to end of row; *4th row* k1 beige, k1 green to end of row; *5th row* join in yellow, k3 beige, k1 yellow to last 2 sts, k2 beige; *6th row* k1 beige, k1 yellow to end of row; *7th row* k1 beige, (k1 yellow, k3 beige) to last st, k1 yellow; *8th row* join in burgundy, k2 burgundy, k1 beige to end of row; *9th row* k1 green, k1 beige to end of row; *10th row* k1 green, k1 beige to end of row; break off green, yellow and burgundy. Cont. in beige only. K1, p1 rib for 4 rows; *15th row* p1 row to reverse stocking top; commencing with a k row, st st for 20 rows. *Commence leg shaping* k1, k2 tog. through back of loops, k to last 3 sts, k2 tog., k1; p1 row; rep. last 2 rows until 24 sts rem.; p1 row. *Commence heel shaping* k6, place sts on safety pin, k12 sts, place last 6 sts onto a safety pin; continue on centre 12 sts for instep; st st for 9 rows; dec. for toe—k1, k2 tog. through back of loops (tbl), k to last 3 sts, k2 tog., k1; p1 row; rep. last 2 rows until 4 sts rem.—k1, k2 tog., k1; p3 tog.; rejoin wool to sts on safety pin; place the 12 sts right side towards you with seam (row ends) in centre, k sts to end of row; p 1 row. *To turn the heel* k6, k2 tog. turn; p1, p2 tog., turn; k2, k2 tog., turn; p3, p2 tog., turn; k4, k2 tog., turn; p5, p2 tog., turn; k6, pick up 6 sts at side of instep at row ends, turn; p12 sts, pick up 6 sts at side of instep and p18 sts; k1 row; p1 row; dec. for instep, k1, k2 tog. tbl, k to last 3 sts, k2 tog. k1; p1 row. Dec. in this manner until 12 sts rem. St st 5 rows; dec. for toe as given for upper foot.

Stitch up side seams and back seam on wrong side with neat oversewing. Turn over top of sock with reversed over-sewing. Make another sock to match.

Jacket Use the same fabric as for the trousers. Paper patterns for the jacket are shown in diagrams 46, 47 and 48. Cut four front pieces (two for front facings in matching fabric), one back and the same in lining fabric, two sleeves, two collars and two pockets. For belt and belt carriers cut four strips of fabric 2 cm (¾ in.) wide by about 24 cm (9¾ in.), another length of the same width to encircle the waist with overlap of 2-3cm (¾-1¼ in.). First, prepare the pockets, belt carriers and belt. Turn over the pocket tops and herringbone to the wrong side, turn over ½ cm (¼ in.) edges to the centre on the belt carriers and belt, tack and press. From now on it is easier to imitate a tailored jacket by machining parts together. Pin the belt carriers to the right sides of the jacket in the position shown, machine stitch in place leaving gaps at the waist for the belt. Stitch the pockets in position. Stitch around the collar, turn to the right side and press. Join the shoulder and side seams, repeat for the lining, press seams open. Pin the collar in position leaving about 1 cm (½ in.) free at either end for revers. Place two jacket pieces right sides together enclosing the collar, machine all round leaving the lower edges open, turn right side out, press, tuck in raw edges and catch closed. Stitch the sleeve seams taking care to have a right and left sleeve. Ease the top of the sleeve with a gathering thread to fit the armhole, match dot to shoulder seam, hand stitch. Turn up the sleeve ends and hem, trim with braid. Cut two pieces of felt or leather for the gun rests (diagram 47) and attach with fabric adhesive. Press the jacket, fasten with small pop fasteners and mock button and buttonholes to the front of the jacket (or make real buttonholes if the fabric is not too thick).

Hats—peaked or soft cap Use the same fabric as for the jacket. Trace the pattern pieces in diagram 44, six cap segments and six in lining

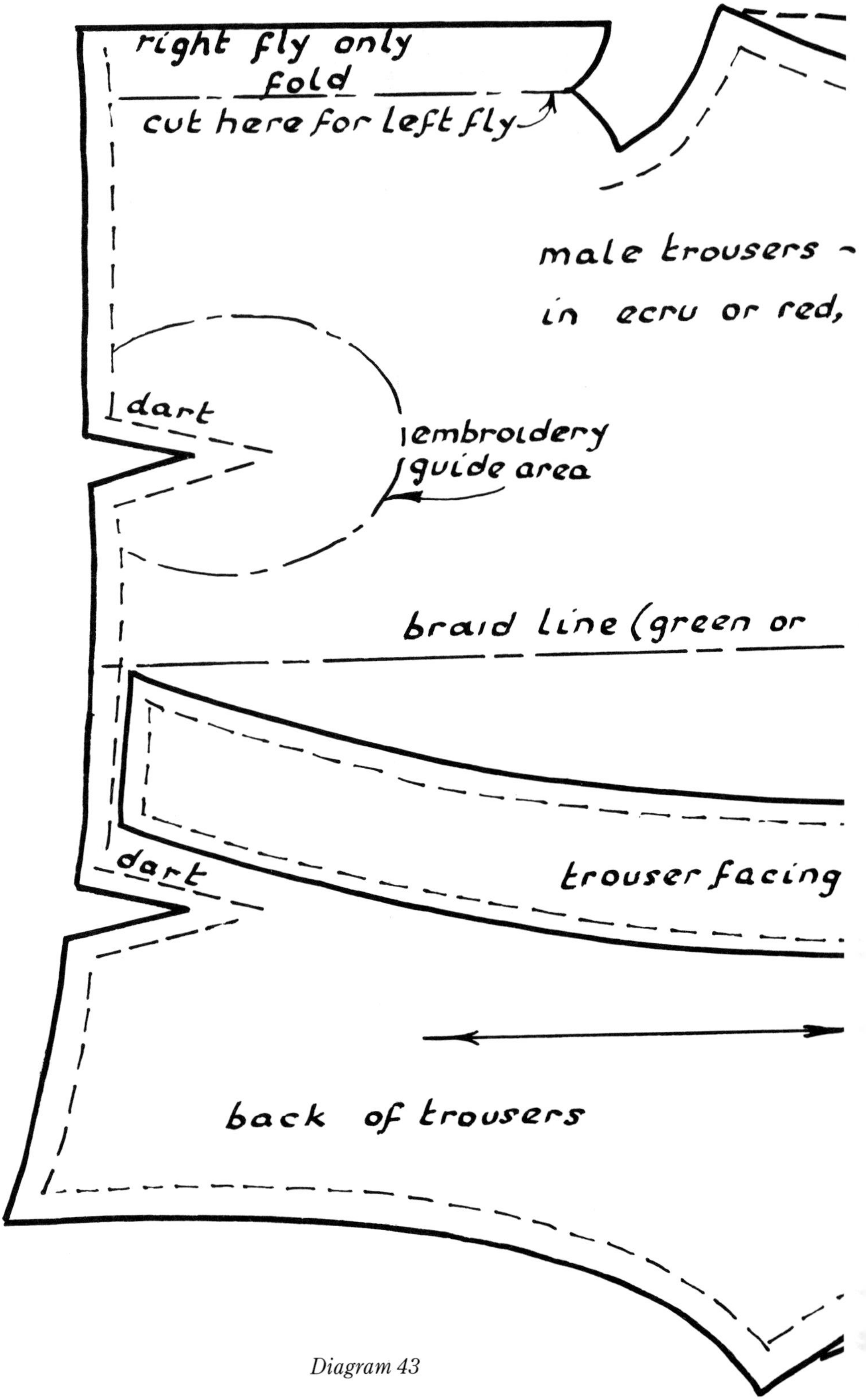

right fly only
_____
fold
_____
cut here for left fly

male trousers ~

in ecru or red,

dart

embroidery
guide area

braid line (green or

dart

trouser facing

back of trousers

Diagram 43

54

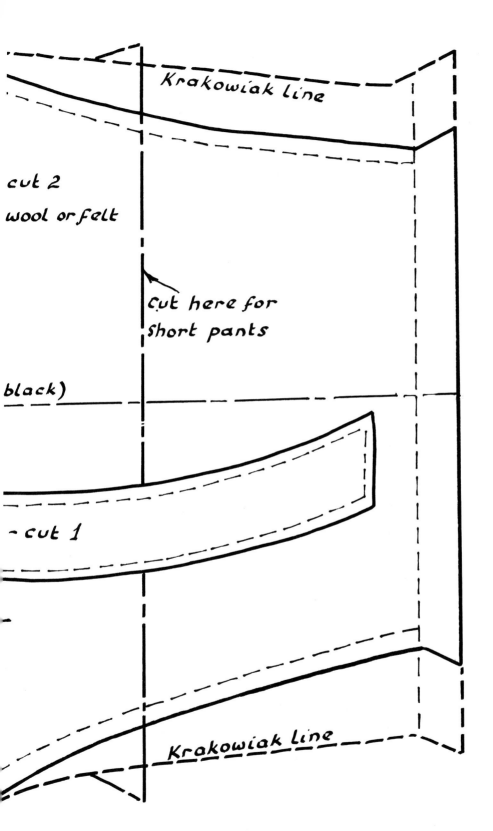

Krakowiak line

cut 2
wool or felt

Cut here for
short pants

black)

- cut 1

Krakowiak line

55

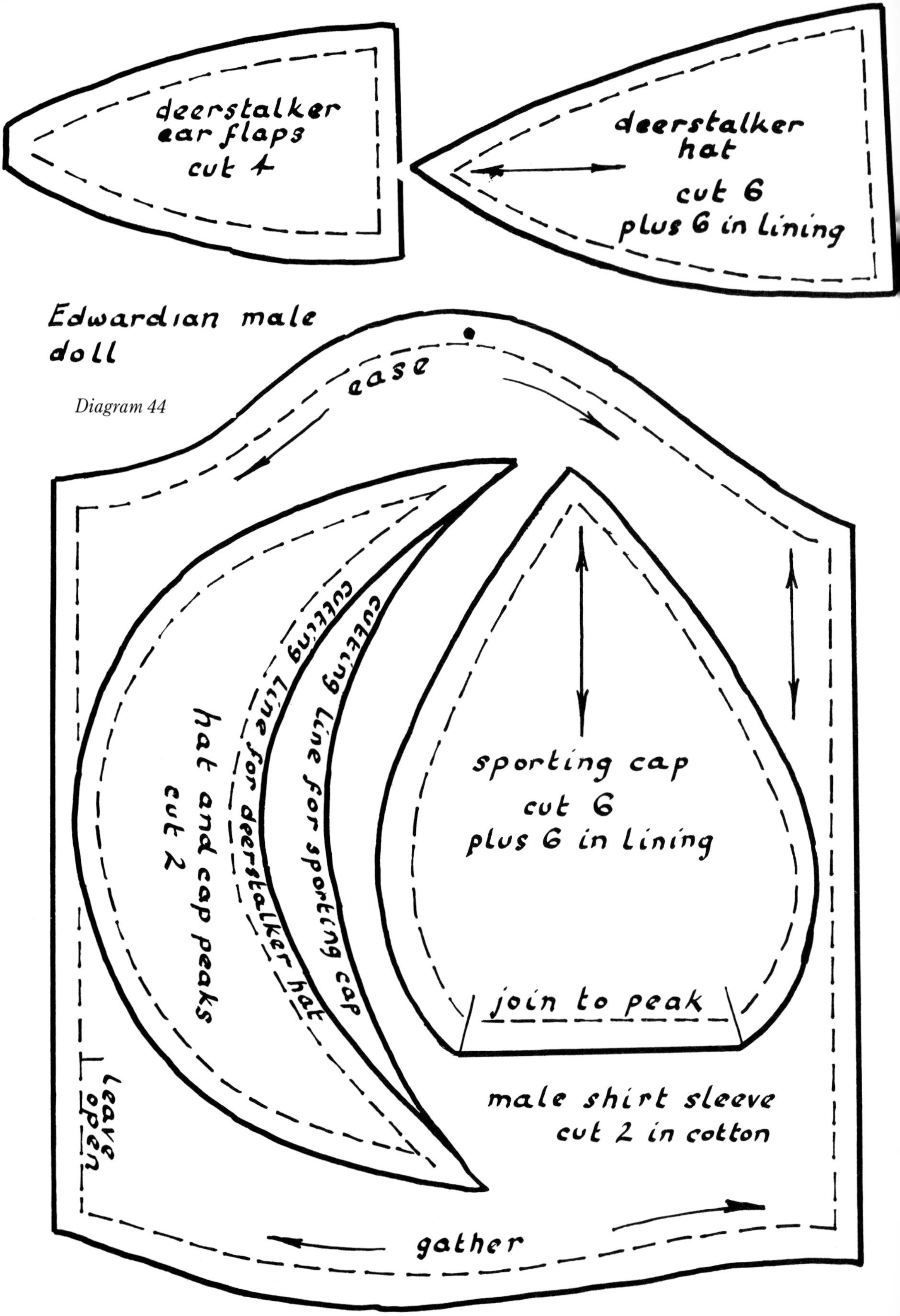

deerstalker
ear flaps
cut 4

deerstalker
hat
cut 6
plus 6 in lining

Edwardian male
doll

Diagram 44

ease

hat and cap peaks
cut 2

cutting line for deerstalker hat

cutting line for sporting cap

sporting cap
cut 6
plus 6 in lining

join to peak

male shirt sleeve
cut 2 in cotton

Leave open

gather

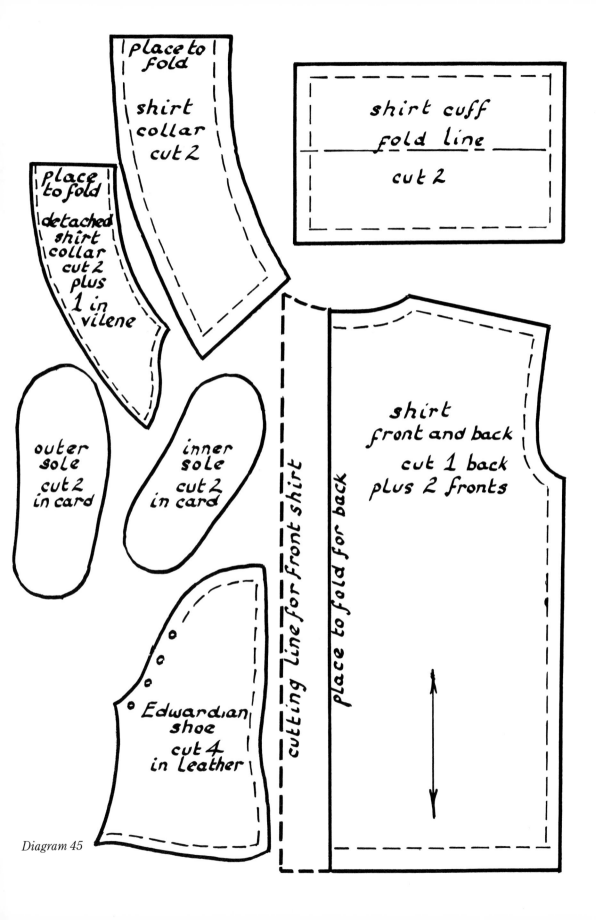

place to fold

shirt collar cut 2

shirt cuff fold line cut 2

place to fold

detached shirt collar cut 2 plus 1 in vilene

outer sole cut 2 in card

inner sole cut 2 in card

cutting line for front shirt

place to fold for back

shirt front and back cut 1 back plus 2 fronts

Edwardian shoe cut 4 in leather

Diagram 45

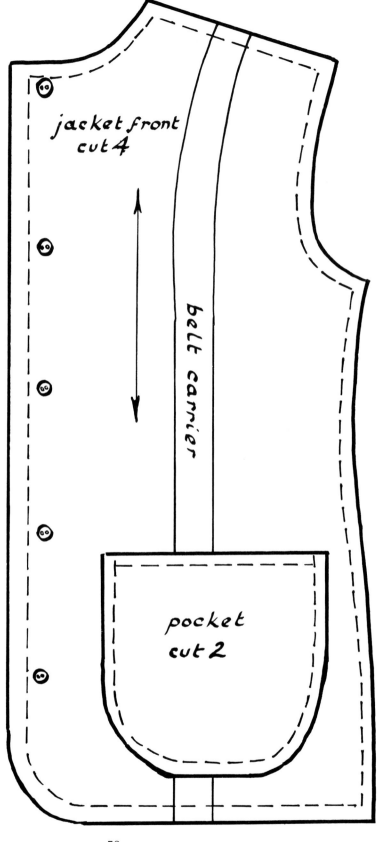

Male Doll
Edwardian sporting jacket

make up in
light wool or
wool/cotton
mixtures –
tiny check or
fleck

jacket front
cut 4

belt carrier

pocket
cut 2

Diagram 46

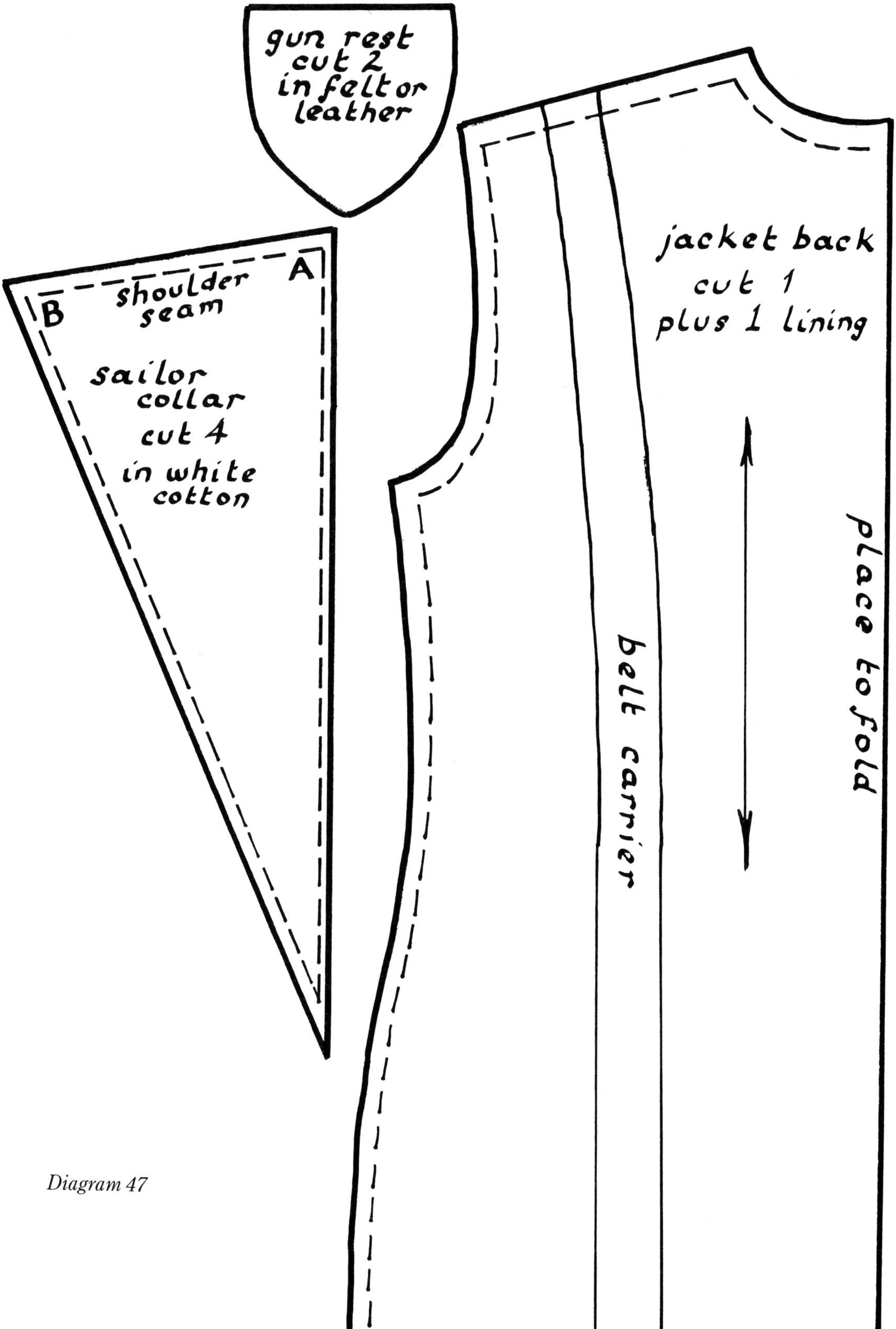

gun rest
cut 2
in felt or
leather

shoulder
seam

B   A

sailor
collar
cut 4
in white
cotton

jacket back
cut 1
plus 1 lining

belt carrier

place to fold

Diagram 47

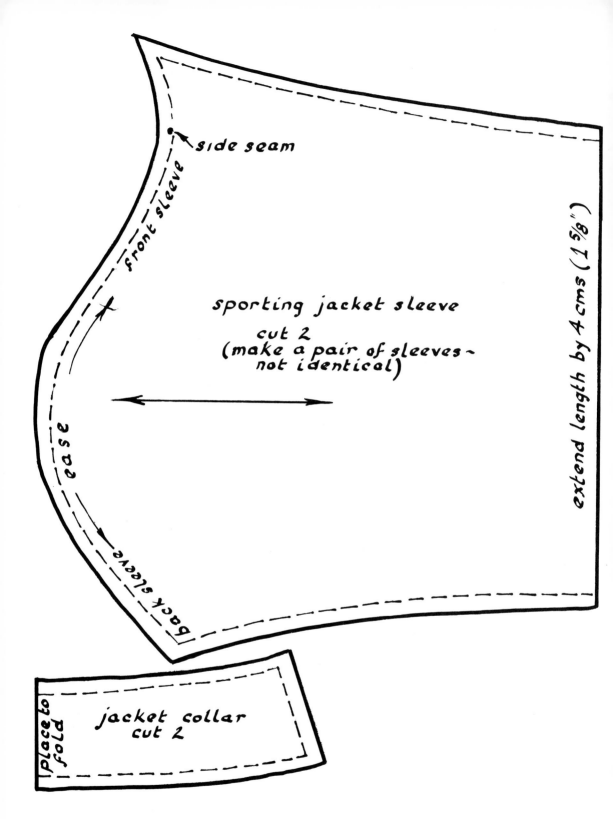

side seam

front sleeve

sporting jacket sleeve
cut 2
(make a pair of sleeves -
not identical)

ease

back sleeve

extend length by 4 cms (1 5/8")

place to fold

jacket collar
cut 2

Diagram 48

fabric, two peaks and one in Vilene. Stitch all the segments together and press the seams open, repeat for the lining. Stitch the two peak pieces together plus the Vilene, turn right side out, trim the Vilene and press. Cut a bias strip in the lining long enough to encircle the head and gather up the edges of the cap to fit. Pin the peak in position and stitch the bias strip over all thicknesses of the cap plus lining, turn the bias to the wrong side and hem. Cover a tiny button with fabric and sew at the centre of the crown to hold lining in position. Block the crown with newspaper and press with a damp cloth. *Deerstalker* (diagram 44). Use fabric and lining as for the cap. Make up as for the cap but using the alternative segments. Cut four brim pieces and two Vilene to the guidelines for the deerstalker and attach to the crown front and back. Add deerstalker flaps over the meeting point of the brims, pin the lining and turn in the raw edges, hem. Press as before. Sew lengths of narrow doll's ribbon to the ends of the ear flaps and tie on top of the head with a bow.

Shoes Cut four shoe pieces in leather (diagram 45). Join the back and front seams, turn right sides out and complete the shoes as described for the child's shoes in Chapter 2.

Edwina (figure 7)

Underwear Pattern pieces for an all-in-one foundation garment are found in diagrams 49 and 50. Use fine white cotton lawn fabric and cut with pinking shears. Join the centre front seam and the back seam as far as the extension for the back opening. Place the front and back right sides together, stitch the shoulder seams and leg seams through the crotch and side seams. Join the neck facings and pin to the neck, gathering in the front neck as required to fit the doll. Stitch and hem to the wrong side. Hem the armholes and trim with lace edging. Turn in the leg ends and hem, trim with lace. Run a length of shirring elastic around the waist and at the leg ends, just below the knee. Sew the buttons amd button loops and the back opening.

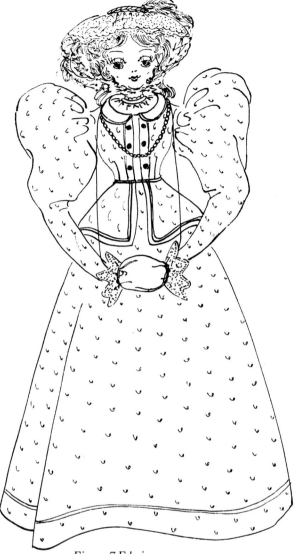

Figure 7 Edwina

Underskirt Using white taffeta for the underskirt, stitch the side seams leaving a small opening to one side for placket (diagram 51). Starched cotton may be used instead of taffeta. Cut a waistband strip 2½ cm (1 in.) wide and long enough to encircle the waist plus 1½ cm (¾ in.). Join the waistband to the skirt, easing in any fullness, turn to the wrong side and hem. Turn up a very narrow hem, trim with lace edging.

Blouse The blouse (diagram 52 and 53) is made of ecru silk and is worn sleeveless if

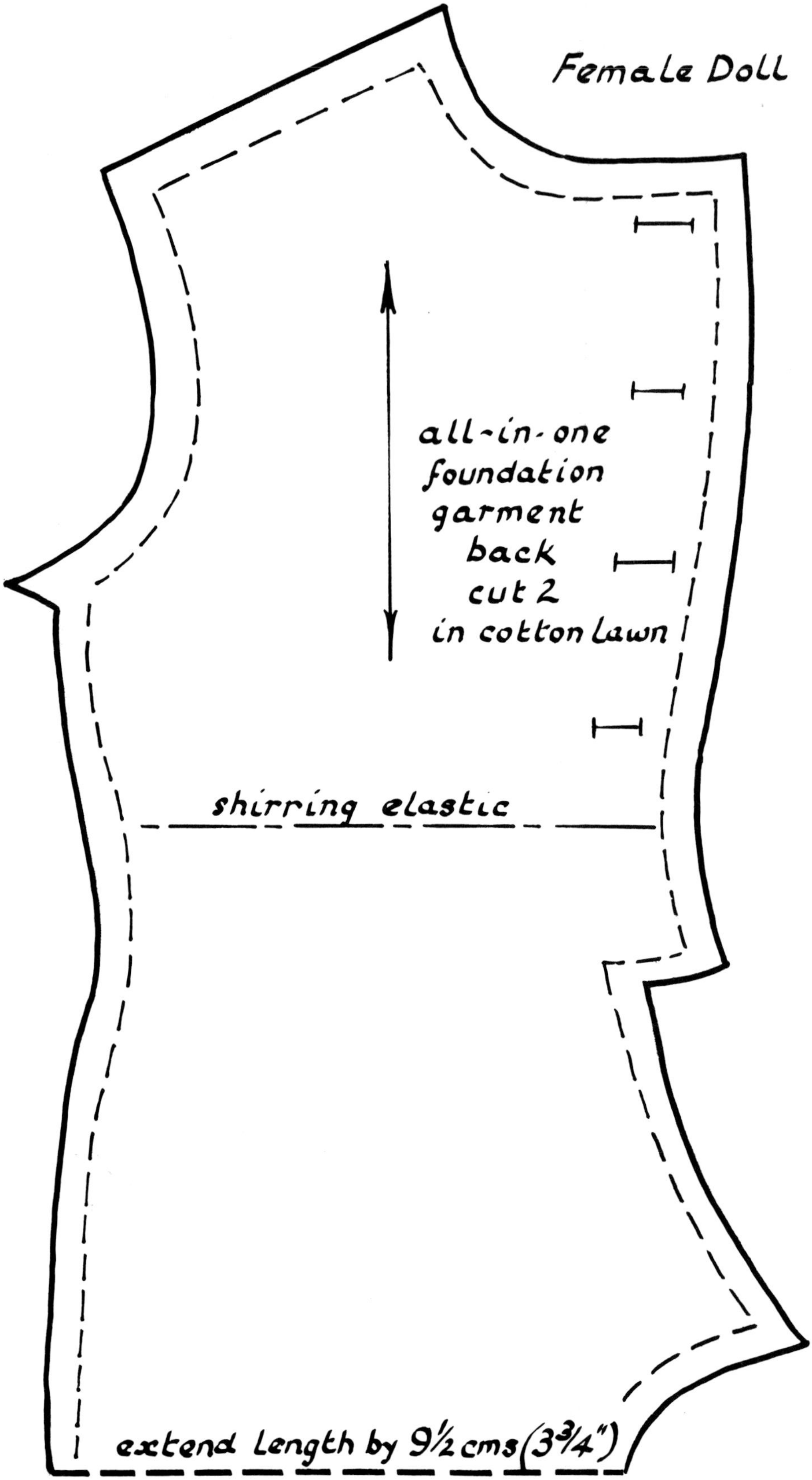

Female Doll

all-in-one
foundation
garment
back
cut 2
in cotton lawn

shirring elastic

extend length by 9½ cms (3¾")

Diagram 49

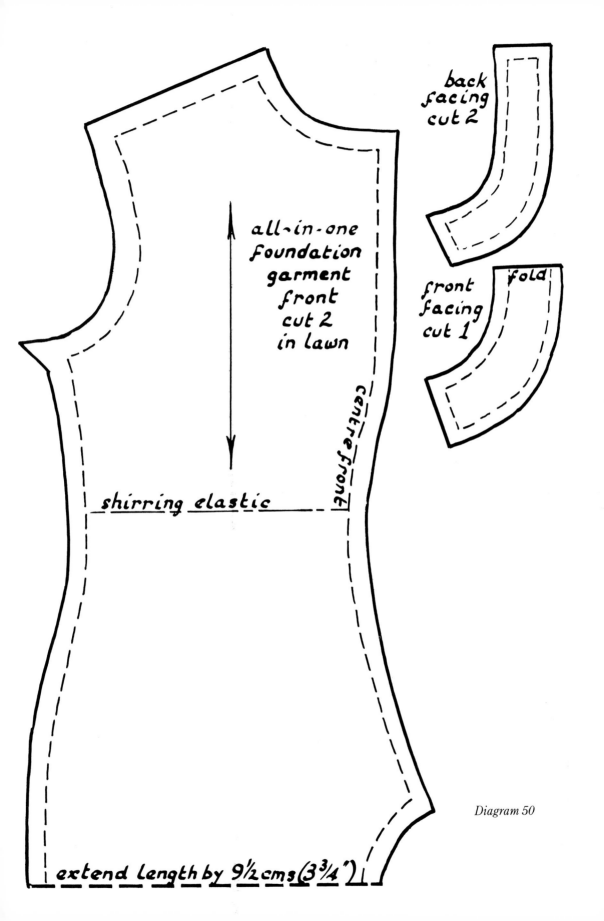

back
facing
cut 2

all-in-one
Foundation
garment
front
cut 2
in lawn

front
facing
cut 1

fold

centre front

shirring elastic

Diagram 50

extend length by 9½ cms (3¾")

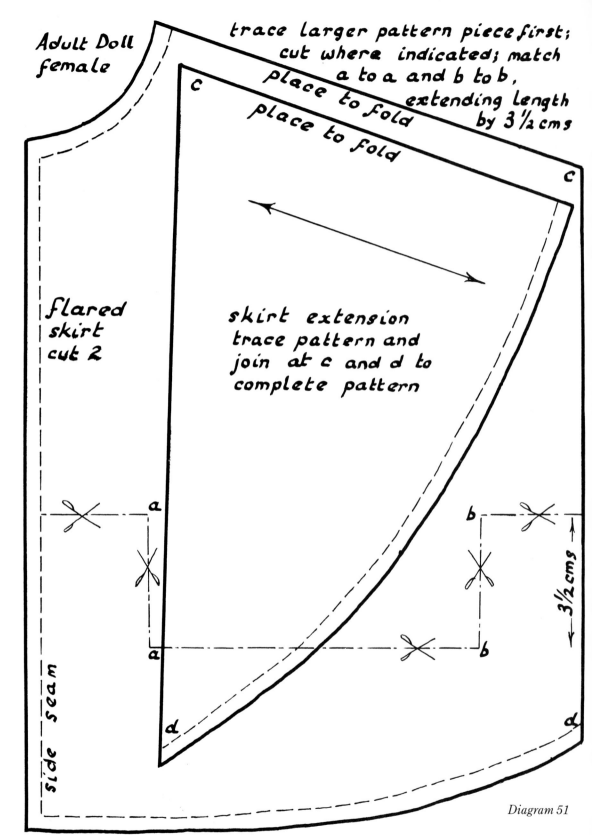

Adult Doll
female

trace larger pattern piece first;
cut where indicated; match
a to a and b to b,
extending length
by 3½ cms

place to fold

place to fold

c

c

flared
skirt
cut 2

skirt extension
trace pattern and
join at c and d to
complete pattern

a

a

b

b

3½ cms

side seam

d

d

Diagram 51

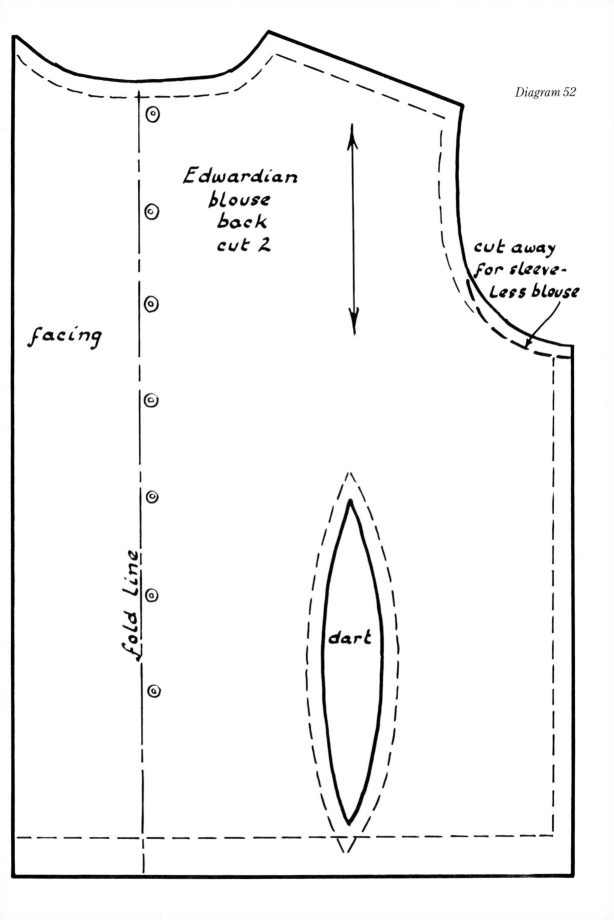

Diagram 52

Edwardian
blouse
back
cut 2

facing

fold line

cut away
for sleeve-
Less blouse

dart

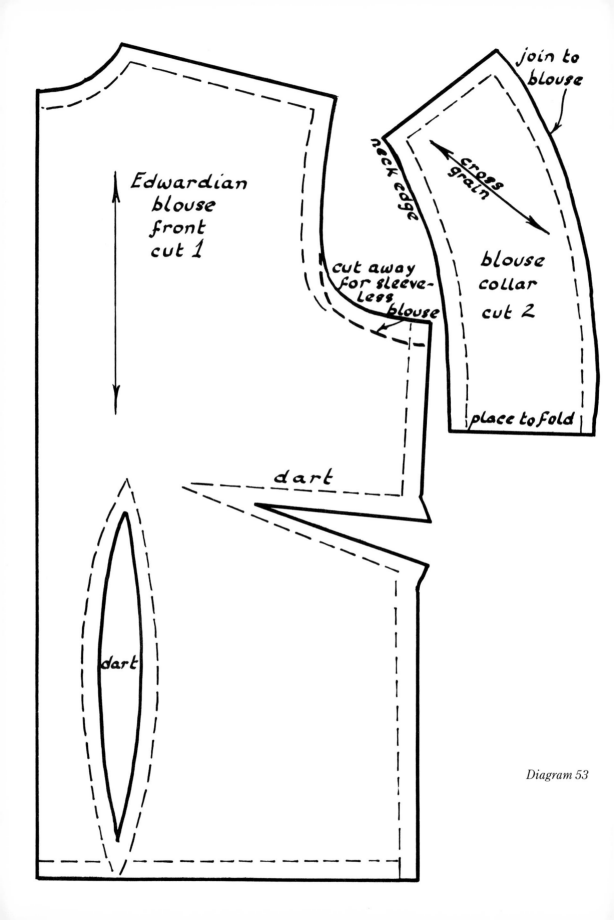

Edwardian
blouse
front
cut 1

cut away
for sleeve-
less
blouse

dart

dart

join to
blouse

neck edge

cross grain

blouse
collar
cut 2

place to fold

Diagram 53

worn under the velveteen jacket. Cut the pieces with pinking shears and stitch the darts to the front and back; turn in the facings and join the shoulder seams. Stitch the two collars together around the three edges, ensuring that they are cut on the bias, as shown. Pin the long edge to the neck of the blouse, stitch and hem to the wrong side. Try on the blouse and adjust the underarm allowance if insufficient. Bind the armholes with bias strip and stitch the side seams. Turn up the lower edge of the blouse and make a narrow hem. Trim the front of the blouse with a lace jabot at the neck. Alternatively, omit the jacket and make a fancy blouse in a sprigged cotton or muslin fabric by the addition of leg o' mutton sleeve cut from the pattern on diagram 54.

Skirt Follow the same instructions as for the underskirt but using velveteen, taffeta or brocade. The appearance is improved by the addition of a bustle (diagram 54). It is made of cotton stuffed with kapok, and is held in place under the skirt by means of ribbon ties.

Jacket This is made from the same fabric as the skirt, pattern pieces are found in diagram 60, using the waistcoat patterns for the Polish dolls with the addition of a peplum and collar (diagram 55). As the waistcoat is intended to be drawn together with lacings, it will be too tight to cover the bosom and extra seam allowance should be allowed at the front seams. Make up the jacket as described for the waistcoat omitting the embroidery, stitching the shoulder and side seams and inserting a leg o' mutton sleeve (diagram 54). Stitch around the collar pieces and turn to the wrong side. Pin to the neck of the jacket leaving the top front of the jacket fronts free, stitch to the jacket with a bias strip turned to the wrong side and hemmed. Trim the jacket with braid and fasten with small buttons and loops.

Boots Make in brown glove leather as described for the child doll's boots inserting a tongue to be held in place with fabric adhesive

(diagram 56). Crochet long laces to match the boots.

Accessories Edwina has two hats, both made from plaited craft raffia, one is a rose colour and the other olive green, both are trimmed with lace and feathers; ready-made hats may also be used. The *parasol* is made with a dowel piece less than ½ cm (¼ in.) in diameter, both ends are sharpened with a pencil sharpener. The tip is wrapped in gold foil and the other end is embedded in a handle made from coloured Fimo clay. The tip of the parasol is passed through a small hole in the centre of a circle of taffeta fabric and fastened in place with thread to the inside of the parasol, concealing the raw edges. Roll the fabric around the parasol in a spiral and hold in place with ribbon or cord. Decorate the top edges with lace to conceal the raw edges. Make a dainty *handkerchief* from a 10 cm (4 in.) square of the finest cotton lawn, make a narrow hem and trim with lace. To make a *muff* cut a length of velveteen or fur fabric 12-15 cm (4¾-6 in.) long and wide enough to encase the doll's hands. Stitch the seam lengthwise, turn the raw ends to the wrong side and herringbone hem, add lace edging. Draw up the muff ends with shirring elastic and add a ribbon of required length to pass round the back of the neck. *Reticule* (diagram 57) cut two bases and one side section in velveteen plus one side in lining, cut a cardboard base. Place the card in the centre of one velveteen base and draw up to cover the card, hold in place with a number of stitches taken from one side to another until the card is secured. Stitch the reticule side ends together, gather the lower edge to fit the base and, on the wrong side, stitch to the right side of the base. Conceal with a second base piece, raw edges turned in and hemmed to the covered card base. Stitch two casing lines near the top of the reticule and make two eyelets on either side. Run a silky cord through the casing with loops to both sides, pass looped ends over the doll's hands. A pearl necklace is made from a packet of pearl beads.

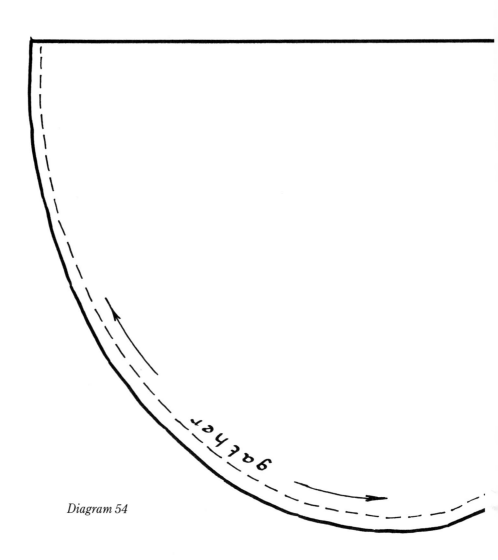

Diagram 54

gather

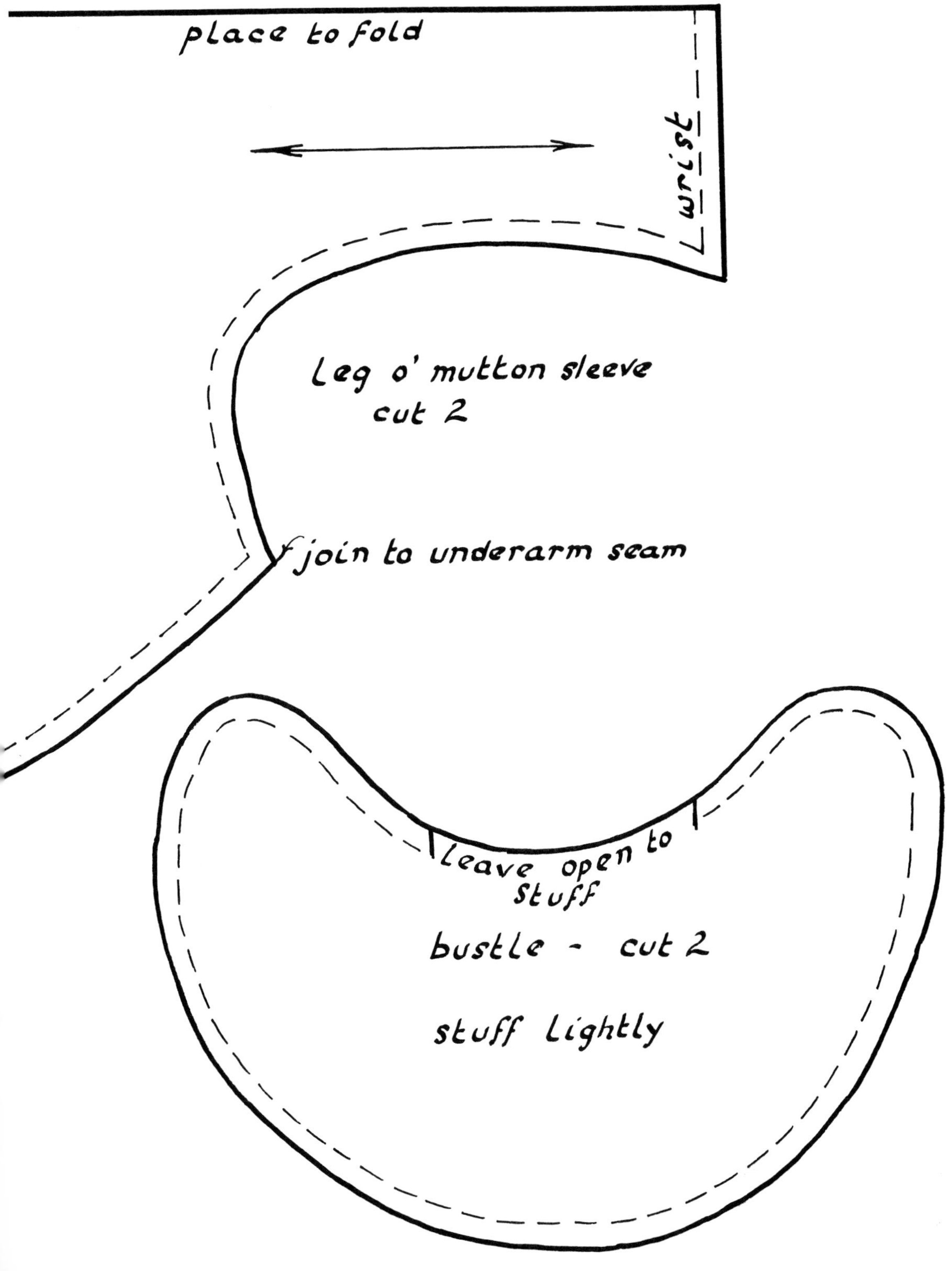

place to fold

wrist

Leg o' mutton sleeve
cut 2

join to underarm seam

Leave open to
stuff

bustle - cut 2

stuff lightly

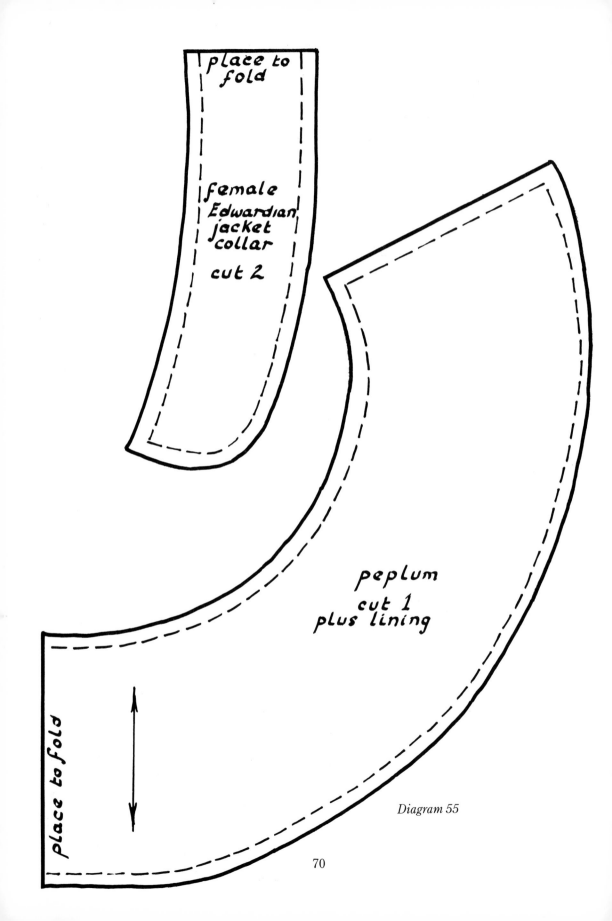

place to
fold

female
Edwardian
jacket
collar

cut 2

peplum
cut 1
plus lining

place to fold

Diagram 55

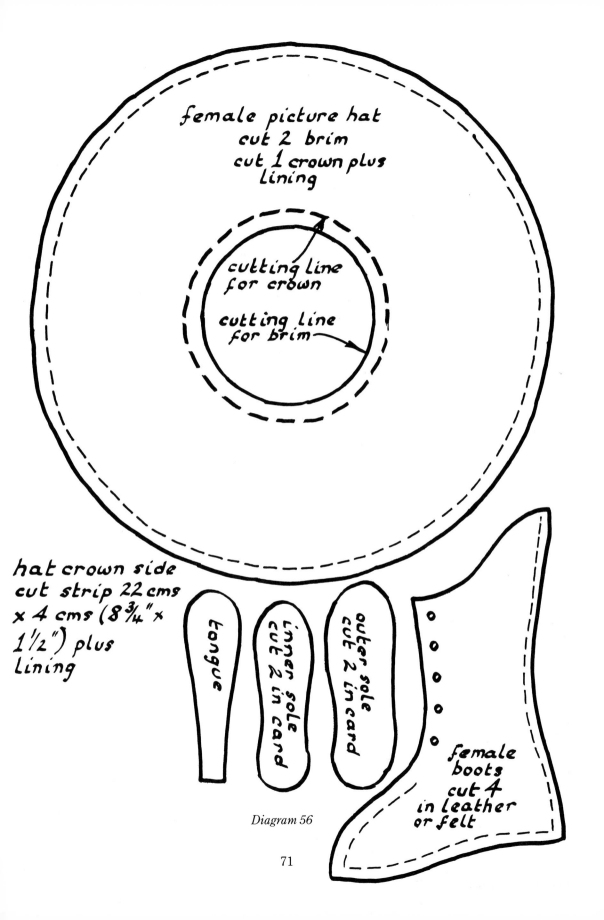

female picture hat
cut 2 brim
cut 1 crown plus
lining

cutting line
for crown

cutting line
for brim

hat crown side
cut strip 22 cms
x 4 cms (8¾" x
1½") plus
lining

tongue

inner sole
cut 2 in card

outer sole
cut 2 in card

female
boots
cut 4
in leather
or felt

Diagram 56

71

female
reticule

base
cut 2

card
base
cut 1

```
┌──────────────────────────────────────────────────────┐
│  ┌─ ── ── ── ── ── ── ── ── ── ── ── ── ── ── ── ──┐  │
│  │                    top                           │  │
│  ├─ ── ── ── ── ── ── ── ── ── ── ── ── ── ── ── ──┤  │
│       stitch and insert draw cord                      │
│  │                                                  │  │
│  │                                                  │  │
│  │        bottom - gather and join to base          │  │
│  └─ ── ── ── ── ── ── ── ── ── ── ── ── ── ── ── ──┘  │
└──────────────────────────────────────────────────────┘
```

Diagram 57

Emma (figure 5)

Emma's bridal or coming-out gown is left to the doll-maker's design. Her underclothes are as for Edwina and include a taffeta underskirt and bustle. Her ecru chiffon dress is made in two parts, blouse and skirt separately for ease of completion and dressing the doll. Edwina's blouse pattern may be used but is worn outside the skirt with a V-shaped front cut. Her sleeves are full and the pattern in diagram 58 was used with increased length and trimmed with a scalloped lace edging.

The *skirt* was made using Edwina's skirt pattern but in two layers, one longer than the other and each heavily trimmed with deep lace. A *bustle* is made from a continuous strip of chiffon some 10 cm (4 in.) deep with an added frill 7 cm (2¾ in.) deep using the selvedge at the lower edge to avoid a cumbersome hem. The length is sufficient to be gathered liberally around the waist and bunched and gathered at the back to hang in gentle gathers over the bustle. Her *shoes* are of soft glove leather and she also wears a string of pearls, and diamonds and emeralds on her fingers (flat glass beads glued to the fingers with clear adhesive). Her hair is a carefully made wig and is decorated with a flower garland.

Arabella (figure 9)

Dress Arabella's dress is chosen to complement her strawberry blonde hair and is made in a soft rose dress-silk or artificial silk. Her *dress* is made in two pieces as for Emma, adapting Edwina's blouse pattern which is tucked inside the skirt. The neck is lace-trimmed and a sleeve cut from the pattern in diagram 58. The skirt is trimmed with pleated sprigged cotton, closely resembling decorations to be seen on some antique dolls. It is made from a long continuous strip (make neat joins in the fabric as necessary) 5 cm (2 in.) wide. Turn in the top and bottom edges to meet at the rear of the frill and press in position along the entire length. With tacking thread pleat the fabric, each pleat lying next to its neighbour, creating double fabric along the length, press. Pin the pleated strip to the narrowly hemmed bottom skirt edge and stitch in position with two rows of

Figure 8 Emma

Figure 9 Arabella

stitching side by side. Add a band of centre lace to conceal the stitching. This edge is time-consuming but well worth the trouble. The dress has a sash of matching fabric with two worked rosettes sewn to it. The *hat* is of rose/gold plaited craft raffia, elaborately trimmed with lace and pink hat feathers (obtained from doll suppliers and some haberdashers). Or make a silk picture-hat from the three pattern pieces shown in diagram 56. Her *boots* are made from buckram and matching rose silk, the pattern used is the same as for Edwina but each piece is cut from buckram and covered in rose silk then made up as described. A raised heel is added by means of a few extra heel sections cut from art-board.

FOUR

National and folk costume dolls

Figure 10 Halina, Zofia and Aniela

Poland

Halina, Zofia and Aniela (figure 10)

Underskirts These are made from starched white cotton. Cut a length 21 cm (8½ in.) by 100 cm (40 in.) and a waistband 3-4 cm (1¼-1¾ in.) wide to fit the waist with an overlap of 1½ cm (¾ in.). Gather one long edge for the waist and draw it up to fit the waistband, stitch the waistband to the skirt, turn to the wrong side and enclose the raw edges in the hem. Join the back seam leaving a small placket opening about 6cm (2¼ in.) long. Add a deep band of broderie anglaise to the hemmed lower edge of the skirt. Fasten with a hook and eye.

Top skirts These should be very bright and colourful, with a predominance of reds, greens, yellows and blacks. Flower patterns should be of a small scale. Make up the skirts as for the underskirt but adjust the length to ensure that the trimming on the underskirt is revealed slightly. If a striped pattern is used, the stripe may be reversed for a horizontal strip at the base of the skirt, adjusting the length of the skirt to remain the same depth overall. See Halina's skirt illustration (figure 10).

Blouse The blouses are made of white cotton lawn. For the pattern pieces see diagrams 59 and 61, Aniela has embroidered sleeves; which are optional, but the embroidery should be completed before the blouse is made up following guide lines on the pattern. Make up the blouse as in diagram 28 with the addition of the collar. Cut two pieces of collar and stitch around three sides, turn to the right side and press. Run a gathering thread around the neck to fit the collar which is worn loose and stands up. Attach the collar as previously described and embroider with several lines of embroidery stitches such as herringbone or feather stitch. Hem the blouse and turn in the facings, run a length of shirring elastic aroud the waist and fasten back with pop fasteners.

Aprons The aprons are of various sizes and ornamentation and are made in white cotton. Cut a rectangle 15-20 cm (8-8 in.) by required depth of the apron. Gather the upper edge of the apron, hem around the apron, trim, with lace, and attach ribbons over the gathered edge, leaving sufficient length either side to fasten in a bow at the back.

Waistcoats The waistcoats are made in dress-weight wool, wool/cotton mixture or felt, in red or black. For the patterns see diagram 60. Cut one back, two fronts and one peplum (diagram 55), plus the same again in lining fabric. Stitch the darts and make up as shown diagram 26. The waistcoats should not meet across the chest but have the lacing stretched slightly. Turn right side out and press. Stitch round three sides of peplum, pin to the waistcoat easing in any bias fullness. On the wrong side conceal the raw edges (diagram 27). If felt is used no lining is necessary but the buttonloops will require reinforcing with a band sewn to the wrong side of the fronts. make button loops to lie in matched pairs at the front of the waistcoats and lace with gold cord or crocheted silk cords. Add gold thread tassels to the front lacing. Embroider the waistcoats with several rows of decorative embroidery to resemble braid or doll zig-zag braid. Zofia has elaborate embroidery on the back and front of the waistcoat plus silk doll braid. See diagram 62 for the design for the embroidery, it should be traced onto the fabric with dressmakers' coloured tracing paper. The embroidery should be completed before assembling the waistcoat, the wrong side of the worked embroidery will then be concealed by the lining. The flowers are worked in satin stitch and the stem and leaves in stem stitch. Use two strands of embroidery thread.

Boots The boots are of red or black leather (diagram 56); if black leather is unobtainable dye with Indian ink and spray with artists' fixative. Complete as for Edwina's boots.

Hair Halina is a brunette. Aniela a blonde, and Zofia has black hair. All have wigs made of

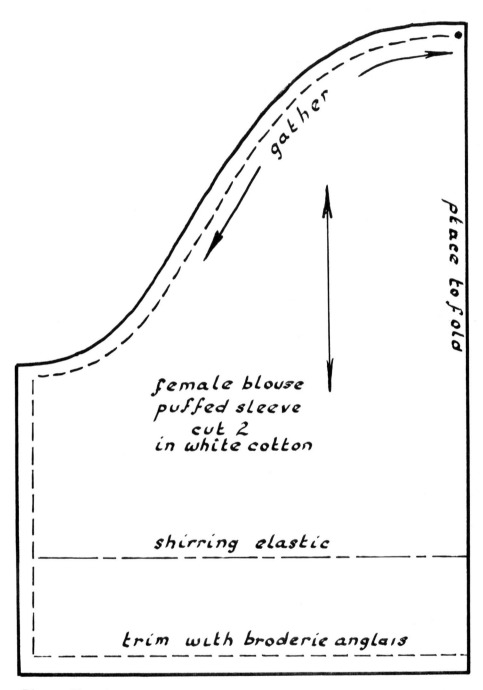

gather

place to fold

female blouse
puffed sleeve
cut 2
in white cotton

shirring elastic

trim with broderie anglais

Diagram 58

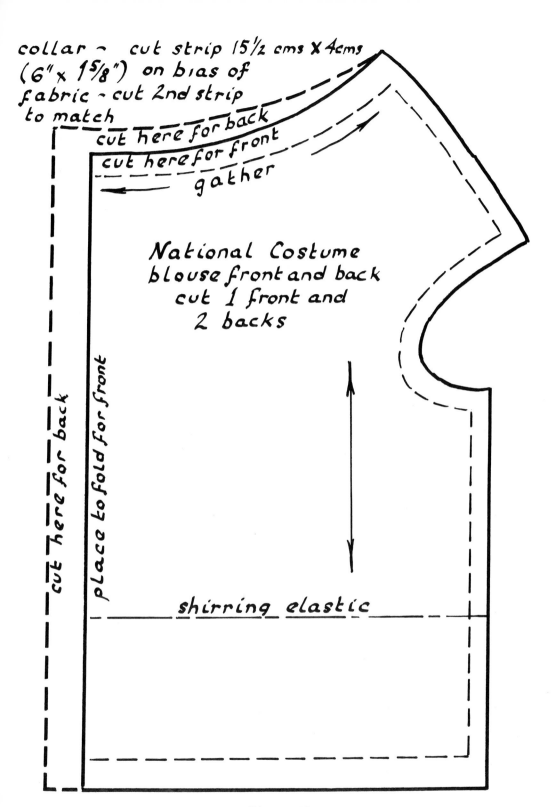

collar ~ cut strip 15½ cms X 4cms
(6" x 1⅝") on bias of
fabric ~ cut 2nd strip
to match

cut here for back
cut here for front
gather

National Costume
blouse front and back
cut 1 front and
2 backs

cut here for back

place to fold for front

shirring elastic

Diagram 59

77

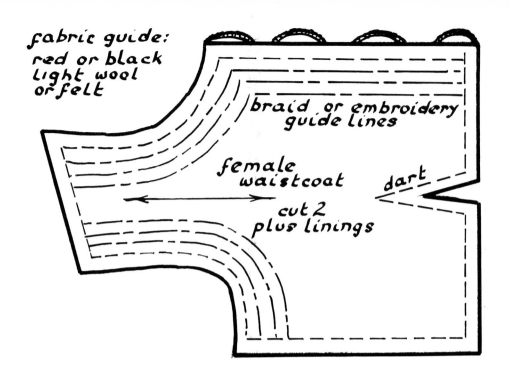

fabric guide:
red or black
light wool
or felt

braid or embroidery
guide lines

female
waistcoat

dart

cut 2
plus linings

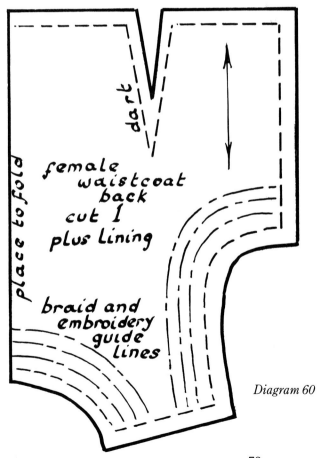

dart

place to fold

female
waistcoat
back
cut 1
plus lining

braid and
embroidery
guide
lines

Diagram 60

78

nylon hair with centre parting and one or two plaits with ribbon bows. A bandeau encircles the hair made of multi-coloured woven braid or ribbon and is adorned with small flowers. These can be obtained from doll specialists or can be grown in the garden from everlasting flower seeds, using only the side shoots and pinching off the smaller buds and blossoms and drying in an airing cupboard.

Jan (figure 11)

Jan is from Krakow. His clothes are made from dress-weight red wool or wool/cotton mixture, and his waistcoat is black. For the waistcoat pattern see diagram 63, the hat pattern diagram 61 the shirt pattern diagrams 45 and 64 and the trousers pattern diagram 43. Using the trouser pattern, make underpants as for Harold.

Shirt Use white cotton lawn. Trace the patterns shown in diagrams 45 and 64 and cut one back, two fronts, two cuffs, two collars and two sleeves. Embroider the full sleeves first on the guide lines indicated, in orange, green and yellow threads. make up the shirt as for Harold, with increased fullness in the sleeve and an attached collar which is also embroidered. Make a bow for a tie in satin ribbon.

Trousers Use red wool fabric and the full-legged pattern cutting on the *Krakoviak* cutting line indicated. Complete as. for Harold but make a simple leg hem and run the elastic through, draw up to calf size. Tuck the trousers into the boots using the pattern in diagram 65 for the boots which are of black leather.

Waistcoat Use black wool, felt or wool/cotton mixture. Trace the patterns and make the waistcoat using the same method as for the Polish girls. Decorate the waistcoat with rows of doll zig-zag braid or rows of embroidery in chain stitch or feather stitch. Make button loops and lace the fronts as before.

Hat This is made from red felt or wool fabric. Trace the pattern shown in diagram 61, cut one

square crown and four side crown pieces. Stitch the angled ends of the crown pieces and pin to the square crown, stitch on the wrong side and turn the right side out and press. Try the hat on the doll and adjust the fit as necessary by varying the angled corner seams. Cut a bias strip in red or black and pin to the hat edge, stretching at the same time for a good fit, stitch and turn to the wrong side and hem. Decorate with small feathers and a bunch of ribbons. Pheasant feathers are very pretty and can be obtained from some butchers.

Stefan (figure 12)

Stefan is a highlander. He wears cream, fitted trousers, cape and waistcoat and a brimmed hat. Use a cream dress-weight or wool/cotton mixture fabric. Make underpants as for Harold, and shirt as for Jan, but with a plain sleeve as for Harold.

Trousers Use the trouser pattern in diagram 43 but cut to the narrower, fitted line. Prior to making up, stitch a length of green doll's braid along the line indicated, taking care to have a left and a right leg. Alternatively embroider a line in chain stitch. Close the darts at the waist. Trace the embroidery motif for the trousers (diagram 66) and transfer it to the fabric where indicated with coloured tracing paper. Work the embroidery and make up the trousers as for Jan with a narrow hem at the ankle.

Waistcoat As for Jan but in a cream wool fabric. Make buttonholes on the left front and sew buttons to the right front.

Cape Use cream wool and matching lining. Trace the pattern pieces, in diagram 67, close the darts and repeat for the lining. Cut out a stand-up collar. Trace and embroider the motif on to the cape fronts. Place the right sides of the cape and lining together and stitch all round leaving the neck free to turn right side out, press. Make up the collar and press, tack to the cape neck and stitch, press in an upright position. Close the neck opening and trim the

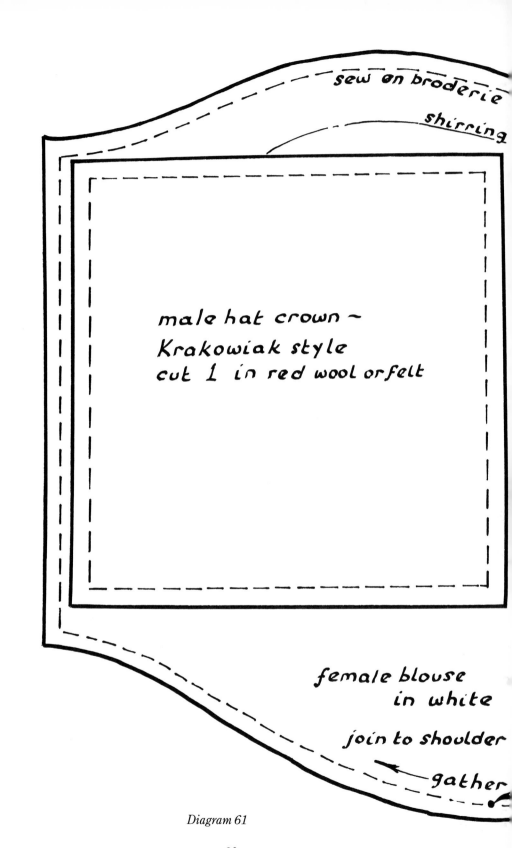

Diagram 61

80

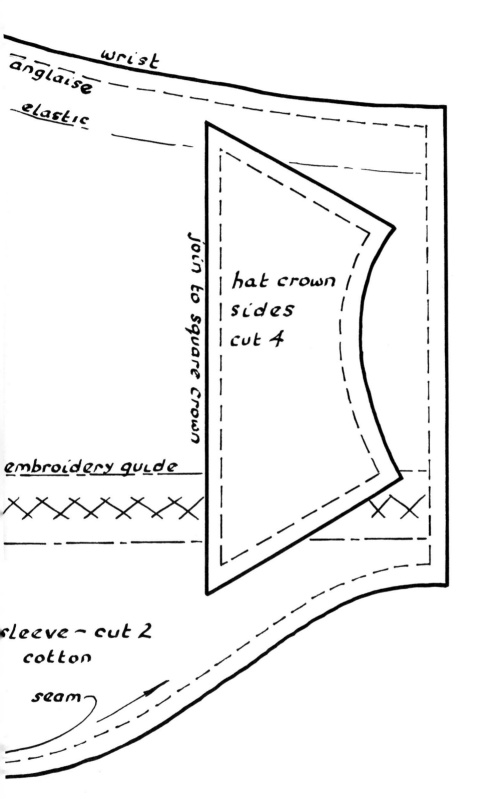

wrist

anglaise

elastic

join to square crown

hat crown
sides
cut 4

embroidery guide

XXXXXXXX   X X X

sleeve – cut 2
cotton

seam

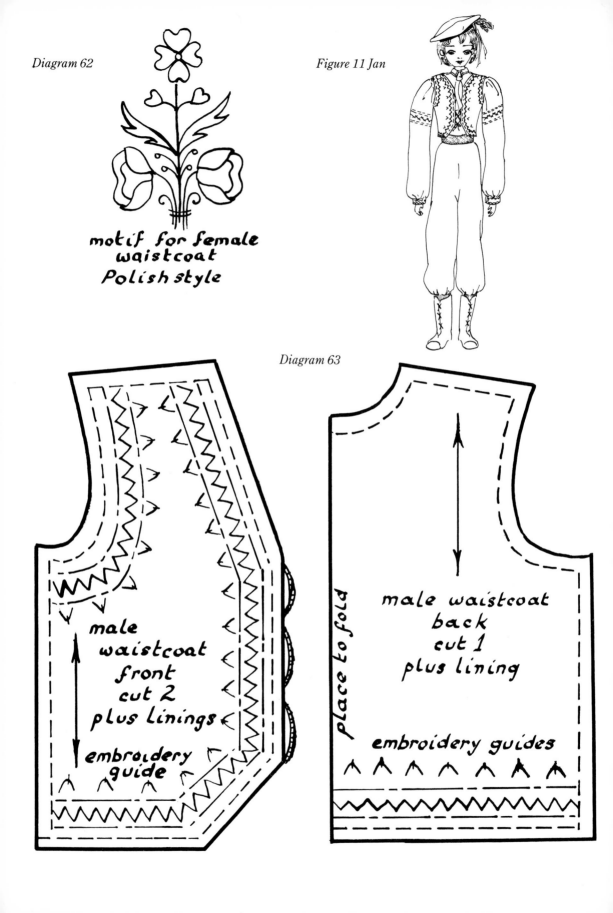

Diagram 62

Figure 11 Jan

motif for female
waistcoat
Polish style

Diagram 63

male
waistcoat
front
cut 2
plus linings

embroidery
guide

place to fold

male waistcoat
back
cut 1
plus lining

embroidery guides

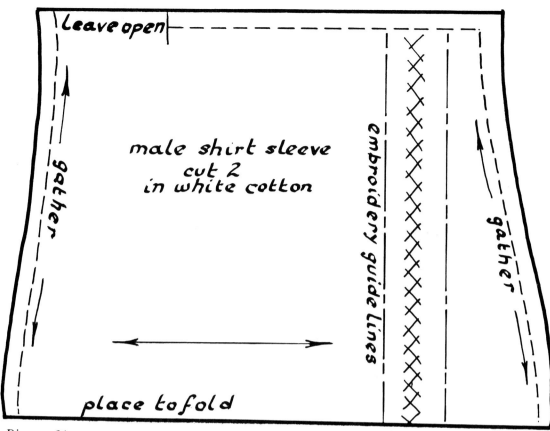

Leave open

gather

male shirt sleeve
cut 2
in white cotton

embroidery guide lines

gather

place to fold

Diagram 64

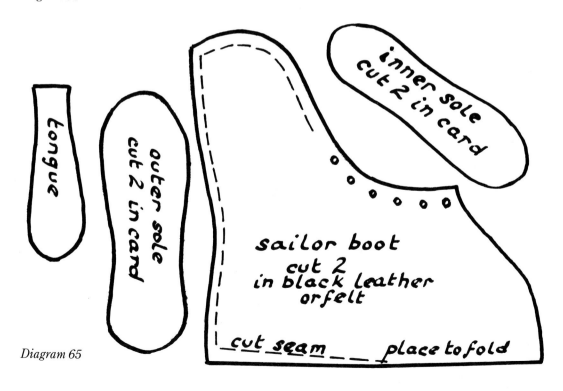

tongue

outer sole
cut 2 in card

inner sole
cut 2 in card

sailor boot
cut 2
in black leather
or felt

cut seam   place to fold

Diagram 65

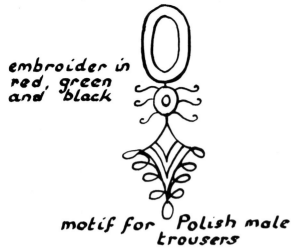

embroider in
red, green
and black

motif for Polish male
trousers

Diagram 66

Figure 12 Stefan

cape with green braid or chain stitch, fasten with a hook and eye.

Hat Make the hat of black felt, using the pattern in diagram 44 as for Harold's hat. Cut six segments, join the seams, check the fit and remove any surplus depth. For a brim use the hat brim shown in diagram 56 but make the diameter less by trimming off the outer circle to a suitable size. Adjust the inner circle to fit the doll's head and attach to the crown with over-sewing to the wrong side, press. Decorate with narrow red braid or ribbon. Trim with feathers.

Boots—as for Jan

Canary Islands

Dolores (figure 13)

Study diagram 42 for the total look. There are many parts to the costume and there is a variation between principal dancers and chorus dancers who have less elaborately embroidered waistcoats.

Underwear and boots As for other female costume dolls. Trim the underskirt with deep broderie anglaise.

Headscarf Use artificial cream silk. Cut a triangle 40 x 40 cm (16 x 16 in.) on the straight edges. Roll the hem very narrowly and oversew. Tie tightly beneath the chin once, pass round to the back of the head, tie again.

Skirt Use a striped fabric, as multi-coloured as possible, but with a predominance of red and black with other bright colours. Cut the fabric length 80-100 cm (32-40 in.) x 22 cm (8¾ in.). Cut the waistband to fit the waist. Complete as for the Polish dolls but ensure that the narrow hem at the lower edge reveals underskirt trimming.

Skirt bobbles Make six tiny wool bobbles from brightly coloured wools. Wind the wool round a

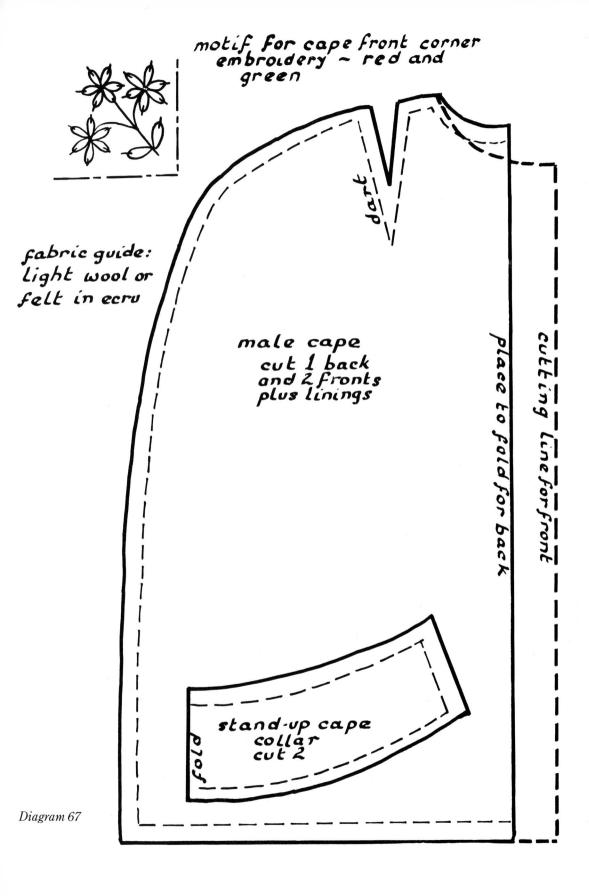

motif for cape front corner
embroidery ~ red and
green

fabric guide:
light wool or
felt in ecru

dart

male cape
cut 1 back
and 2 fronts
plus linings

place to fold for back

cutting line for front

stand-up cape
collar
cut 2

fold

Diagram 67

Figure 13 Dolores

lolly stick many times, fasten all the loops together with a strand of the same colour wool passed beneath the loops, draw the thread tightly and fasten off securely. Remove the wool loops from the stick and trim the ball with sharp scissors to a smooth, round shape. Crochet matching chain lengths and attach to the balls. Tie the chains together so that the balls fall at varied lengths, revealing all the colours. Make a loop at the end of the chain and attach the chain to both sides of the skirt in such a manner as to draw up one side of skirt to reveal the underskirt.

Blouse Make in white cotton lawn, as for the Polish blouses but substituting the sleeve shown in diagram 58. Attach the broderie anglaise trimming below the elbow. Change the collar style to a gathered neck with a bias strip added. Trim the neck with broderie anglaise.

Apron Use white cotton lawn fabric and the pattern in diagram 68. Cut out the necessary pieces, tack the narrow hem round the pockets and trim with narrow broderie anglaise. Stitch the pockets to the apron, leaving the trimming

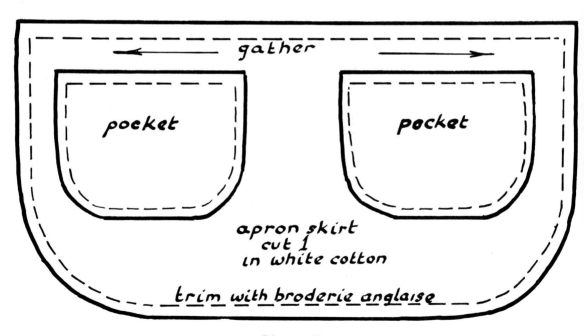

Diagram 68

to frill freely. Stitch on wider trimming around the outer edge of the apron, draw up to fit the waist and stitch to the ribbon acting as waistband and ribbon ties.

Chorus girl waistcoat This is made in black wool or felt. Cut strips of red bias binding from the lining fabric. The pattern for the waistcoat is shown in diagram 60. Make up as for the Polish waistcoats but omit peplum and substitute eight tabs. Cut eight tabs (diagram 69) in black fabric and pin them to the waist edge by the straight edge, stitch and press the seam. With a continuous strip of red bias binding pin and stitch around all the edges of the waistcoat, treating each tab individually. Turn the bias to the wrong side and hem neatly. Add button loops and a crochet cord and lace the waistcoat.

Principal girl's waistcoat This is made in red wool or felt. Use the pattern given on diagram 69 for the back and two fronts and eight tabs. Additionally, cut a strip of fabric 2 cm (¾ in.) wide by 15 cm (6 in.) long. Line the waistcoat with matching fabric if desired. Close the darts at the front and the back and attach the tabs as described above. Cut a continuous strip of gold acetate bias binding. Join the side seams for both waistcoat and lining. Bind all round the waistcoat, as previously described, and also both long edges of the red strip. Divide the strip evenly in half for the shoulder straps and stitch an end to the wrong side of the back of the waistcoat. Try the garment on the doll and pin the position for the front shoulder strap, adjusting the length as necessary. Embroider the entire garment as indicated on the pattern in gold, green and yellow embroidery threads. Use stem and feather stitches with lazy daisy loops and green dash stitches representing corn stems, then fly stitching at the top edge of the waistcoat interspersed with dash stitches (diagram 28).

Cape The cape is made from green felt and edged with gold bias binding. It is always worn over the shoulder as shown. Cut a rectangle 28 x 17 cm (11¼ x 6¾ in.) and gather one long edge. Cut the cape band from the pattern on diagram 70, fold in half, and stitch one side to the cape and hem the other. Bind all the edges with gold bias. Sew the ribbon ties to the neck of the cape.

Hat The hat is of natural straw, plaited, and stitched together, with the edge bound in red bias. Alternatively, purchase a ready-made hat in a size too small. The hat is worn at a rakish angle by means of elastic at the back of the head or tied with red ribbons.

Yemen

Said (figure 14)

He is dressed as a bearer or waiter. He wears cotton pants as for the other male dolls and a white shirt as for Harold with an open neck. He does not wear trousers, unless prescribed at his place of work. He prefers to wear the traditional, loose garment wrapped around the waist. Using a small check cotton, cut a piece 45 cm (18 in.) long by 25 cm (10 in.) wide with the selvedge to the lower edge if possible, if not—hem narrowly. Turn the waist edge over and wrap the length around the doll with the front edge folded into the waist. When in Arab company Said will wear the traditional *head-dress* made from a square of white cotton, narrowly hemmed, about 23 cm (9¼ in.) square. This type of head-dress is held in place with black silk cords, doubled and caught together at four corners. A shoe lace will suffice for a cord. When working as a waiter, Said is likely to wear the Turkish *fez* which is made from red felt and heavyweight Vilene. Cut a length of Vilene long enough to encircle the head and 5 cm (2 in.) deep. Pin the short ends, then cut out four or five darts from the top crown edge, petering out at the lower edge. Stitch the darts closed and cut a circle in Vilene to fit the top crown. In red felt cut out matching pieces with a seam allowance and overlapping edges. Attach the felt to the Vilene with fabric adhesive and when dry, hem the felt over the edges or trim neatly and stitch the side seam.

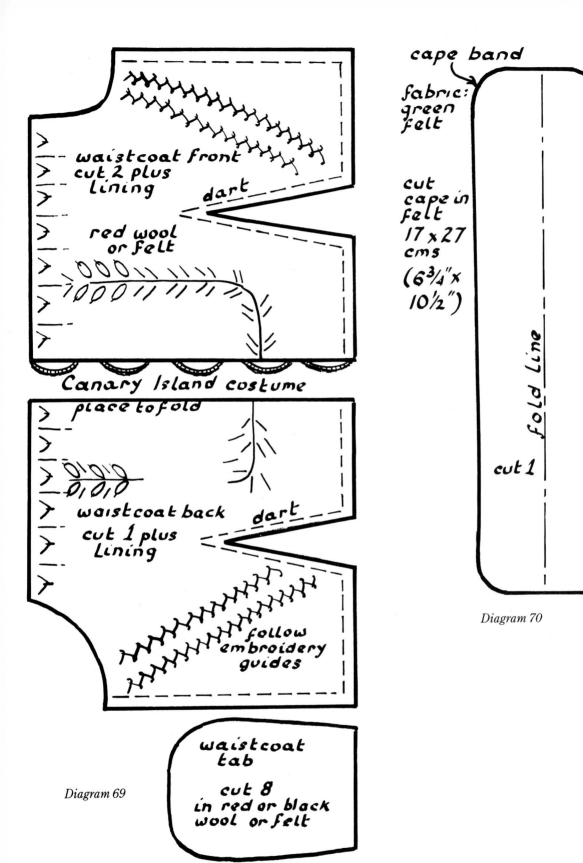

waistcoat front
cut 2 plus
lining

dart

red wool
or felt

Canary Island costume

place to fold

waistcoat back
cut 1 plus
lining

dart

follow
embroidery
guides

Diagram 69

waistcoat
tab

cut 8
in red or black
wool or felt

cape band

fabric:
green
felt

cut
cape in
felt
17 x 27
cms
(6¾"x
10½")

Fold Line

cut 1

Diagram 70

Figure 14 Said

Add a black tassel made from embroidery threads and fasten to the centre of the crown top. Said wears brown shoes, as for Harold.

Red Indian

Geronimo (figure 15)

Geronimo is a Red Indian brave. His outfit is made using the basic shirt, trouser and waistcoat patterns. His *pants* are white cotton, and brown *shirt* is collarless with bound neck and the *waistcoat* and *trousers* are made from real brown suede, or imitation suede cloth may be used. Use fabric adhesive to hem the fly fronts but stitch the other seams. The ankle edges are fringed with scissors and a separate belt of narrow leather strip with a gilt buckle is added. The elongated waistcoat is also fringed and a mock fringed yoke is added with fabric adhesive. The warrior *headband* consists of two pieces of felt cut to the size of the head circumference, glued together to enclose a collection of graded feathers, highest to the centre. The band is then decorated with braid or embroidery. Alternatively, he wears a *fur hat* of simple construction which is a band of rabbit fur encircling the head and a round section cut to fit crown. Fur fabric is also suitable. Around his neck he wears a rope of assorted wooden beads and a neckerchief made from a square of red cotton fabric, narrowly hemmed and measuring about 25 cm (10 in.) square. On his feet he wears *moccasins;* first trace the foot size and cut cardboard soles to the same measurement. Now cut a leather 'U' shape straight at the heel but curving round the foot size by an additional 1½ cm (¾ in.) longer and wider than the foot. Glue the cardboard inner sole to the wrong side of the leather and stitch up the back seam at the heel. Run a gathering thread around the 'U' shape and draw it in to fit the foot. Cut a smaller 'U' shape to fit the front of the shoe and stitch it to the shoe on the outside. Embroider the moccasin on the front.

Figure 15 Geronimo

Figure 16 Marie and Pierre

France

Marie (figure 16)

Marie's undergarments are as for the other dolls mentioned. Her *dress* is made in two parts, blouse and skirt separately. The fabrics are red and black cotton. The skirt is made from red cotton 100 cm (40 in.) long by 28 cm (11¼ in.) deep with a waistband 4 cm (1¾ in.) wide and 2 cm (¾ in.) longer than the circumference of the waist. The skirt is worn ankle length and decorated with bands of braid and lace. The bodice is made from Edwina's blouse pattern but the sleeves are an adaptation of Harold's shirt sleeve; cut straight at the wrist with added length as necessary. The sleeves are trimmed with many rows and layers of gathered lace and satin ribbon. Prior to assembling the blouse a contrasting 'V' piece of fabric is stitched to the front of the blouse bodice, the stitching is then concealed with a frilled band of lace commencing at centre front and passing over the shoulders to meet at the centre back. The *apron*, as for other dolls, may be pastel or jewel coloured with a frilled lace edging. The *lace head-dress* is very elaborate and is supported by a crescent of heavyweight Vilene hidden beneath layers of starched and ruffled lace stitched to both sides. It is attached to the hair which is dressed in a centre parting, looped over the ears, and twisted into a coil at the nape of the neck which helps to support the head-dress. The *boots* are as for the other costume dolls and may be brown or black leather.

Pierre (figure 16)

His *undershirt* is made from narrowly candy-striped blue/white fabric and is sleeveless. Harold's shirt pattern is used with the fastening reversed to the back and there is no neck shaping. The front and backs are cut straight across from one shoulder to the other and narrowly hemmed and caught together at the shoulders. The arm holes are cut deeper and faced with bias strip. A pattern is given for the sailor collar in diagram 71 and it is made up in dark blue and white fabric as indicated. Stitch the collar fronts to the sloping shoulders of the back collar and repeat for a second set, then stitch the narrow bands of white ribbon to the back collar of one set. Place the right sides together and stitch all round the two collar sections, leaving a small opening at the back of neck for turning right side out. Close the opening and stitch the collar to the jerkin top.

For the *jerkin*, again use the shirt pattern with added seam allowance and two identical pieces for the front and back. Suitable fabrics are navy felt, light wools or wool/cotton mixture. Alternatively, use a discarded navy wool sweater for greater flexibility when dressing the doll, navy wool socks can be made from lengths of ribbed welt from the same sweater. From the shoulders at the front of the jerkin, cut a 'V' opening, deep enough to match the collar, and conceal the stitching at the collar

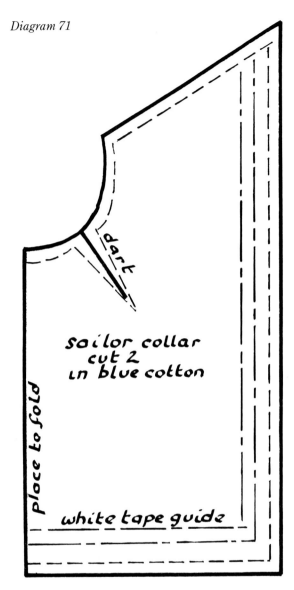

Diagram 71

sailor collar
cut 2
in blue cotton

place to fold

white tape guide

and hem. Decorate the hat with a red pom-pom and bands of ribbon. The *trousers* are cut from diagram 43 on the *Krakoviak* line, full length, and of navy felt or wool. See diagram 65 for the pattern for the black boots.

Dye leather with Indian ink and spray with fixative if black leather is not available.

Japan

Madame Butterfly (figure 17)

Madame Butterfly is the most difficult doll to dress and left to the end of the book for that reason. Her skin colour is pale, almost white, and her eyelashes are artificial. Dolls' lashes can be purchased at specialist shops, one pair is sufficient for two dolls as only half a lash is used at a time. Her hair is wavy black mohair and is stitched to a wig base and a black bias strip in every decreasing circles, commencing at the edge of the wig base. Gently brush the hair and arrange it in coils, commencing at the centre and working outwards; each grouping of hair is secured with matching thread.

The underclothing is the same as for all other female dolls. She wears a wrap-round red tricel underskirt made from one length of fabric approximately 33 cm (13¼ in.) long by 22 cm (8¾ in.) deep and narrowing at the hem at the ankle. On the wrong side make two darts at the waist front and two at the back, each set evenly spaced from centre front and centre back. Wrap the underskirt around the doll with the overlap at the back and secure with a hook and eye. Stitch two or three more sets of fastenings evenly spaced to hem, increasing the wrap over as you do so, creating a slightly hobbled skirt. Next, make a provisional paper pattern for the kimono out of newspapers. Two full sheets will be required. Take one folded sheet and spread on a table with the folded edge uppermost on a horizontal line. On that same line, lay the doll with arms fully stretched outwards at the shoulder level, placing the doll slightly below the fold to allow for the fold to match the centre shoulder of the doll. Measure

ends with a black ribbon bow. The sleeves are as for Harold's shirt but with increased length and cut straight. Stitch the side and shoulder seams.

The *beret* is made from felt or sweater fabric used double thickness. Using the pattern shown in diagram 56, cut two circles in navy at the outer circumference and remove an inner circle on one piece to fit the head. Stitch the outer edges and turn right side out. Cut a 4 cm 1¾ in.) wide strip to fit the head and stitch to the edge of the beret, turn to the wrong side from the shoulder to the ankle of the doll, transfer the measurement to newspaper and cut off the bottom surplus. Similarly measure from one wrist to another of outstretched arms and cut off surplus at either side. Measure the hips from one centre hip to the other and allow some additional seam allowance for freedom of movement as a kimono is worn fairly loose. Transfer this measurement to the newspaper. (At this time it is advisable to make a central vertical crease in the newspaper from which to space all measurements evenly at either side). Mark the hip measurement on paper and cut up vertically from ankle to arm-pit (allowing for a deep arm-hole) through two thicknesses of

Figure 17 Madame Butterfly

paper and on both sides of the hips. The sleeves of a kimono are also deep pockets, almost as long as the garment itself. Remove about one third of the depth of the sleeve pocket. Now cut the pattern in half vertically through the centre crease line, retain one half of the pattern as a guide for the final pattern but discard the second half as unnecessary. Scoop out the front and back neck to fit the doll. Now make the final pattern. Open out a second sheet of newspaper and also open out the halved pattern piece; lay it on the second sheet. Now adjust the front slope of the pattern to make a wrap-over style. Extend the front edge from neck to waist in a gentle curve, mark the new shape on paper with a pencil and extend the pencil line to the hem in a straight line. Cut out the final paper pattern to a new shape and discard the first trial pattern. Try the half pattern on the doll and adjust as necessary. Once satisfied of a good, loose fit, use the pattern for cutting the chosen fabric for the kimono. Suggested fabrics are flowered silk, georgette, or some types of silky cottons. Use a jewel-coloured tricel fabric for the facings. Use the paper pattern to cut two matching front facings to the same size as the fronts of the kimono; two facings for the sleeves at wrist about 5 cm (2 in.) wide, and 2½ cm (1 in.) wide for the back and front ankle hems and also at the back of the neck. Now lay the paper pattern onto the floral silk with the front edge to the straight grain of the fabric. Cut out two identical pieces. Stitch together the centre back seam and stitch facings to the right side of the front pieces, turn these to the wrong side and press lightly. Repeat with the sleeve facings, neck facing and hems. With right sides together, stitch side seams to armpits, down sleeve pocket seams and across the bottom of them and up towards wrist, leaving a very loose sleeve with exposed facings. Lightly press the kimono and dress the doll using a pop fastener at the waist to hold the fronts in a wrap-over style. Make a sash from brocade. As brocade is an expensive fabric it may be lined with tricel. The sash is a strip 7 cm (2¾ in.) wide and long enough to encircle the waist with small overlap, the same in lining. With right sides together, stitch two long and one short side, turn to the right side and press; close with a hook and eye. Make a mock bow at the back with a lined strip of brocade 12 cm (4¾ in.) wide by 30 cms (12 in.) long. Join the folded strip to the back sash with a small piece of brocade placed across the fold, edges turned in, and stitched in place. The sash is decorated with rose buds and jewels, as is the hair. A fold of cream silk inside the neck of the kimono makes a cravat fastened with a pop fastener. Cover the legs in white stockings. The sandals have platform soles made from five to six stacked layers of art-board soles cut to the shape of the bottom of the foot and glued together in a tier. The soles are then covered in fabric and invisibly hemmed, straps are made from cream silk.

Madame Butterfly completes the number of costume dolls in this book but many more can be made by studying costume at museums, visiting other lands, and reading books on the subject. Two useful books are: *Folk Costumes of the World,* published by Blandford, and *The Folk Dress of Europe* by James Snowden, published by Bell & Hymen.

Many other adaptations are also possible using the paper patterns in this book. Boys might prefer 'Action Man' dolls; camouflage combat outfits can be made by adapting the adult male patterns and using khaki, air force blue, or navy fabric; sweater fabric can be substituted for shirts with shoulder rein-forcements, etc.

SUPPLIERS

Fred Aldous Ltd, P.O. Box 135, 37 Lever St, Manchester M60 1UX-*most handicraft supplies*

Dryad, P.O. Box 38, Northgates, Leicester, LE1 9BU or at 178 Kensington High St, London-*handicrafts, artists' materials, Das and Fimo clays*

The Handicraft Shop, 47 Northgate, Canterbury, Kent-*many craft items including Fimo and Das clay, polystyrene balls*

Handicraft Materials, 134 Montague Street, Worthing BN11 3HG-*handicraft items, polystyrene balls, Fimo and Das clay*

Hullo Dolly, Dolls Hospital, Gwavas Lane, Newlyn, Penzance, Cornwall TR18 5NA-*doll kits, hats, shoes, wigs, tiny buttons etc.*

John Lewis, Oxford Street, London-*fabrics of all kinds including craft fabrics*

Liberty and Co Ltd, Regent Street, London W1R 6BA-*suede and glove leather*

The Model Shop, Castle Street, Truro, Cornwall-*handicrafts, artists' materials, Fimo and Das clay*

Prickwillow, Margo & Derek Andrews, 52 Main St., Prickwillow, Ely CB7 4UN-*doll kits*

Recollect, 82c Trafalgar Street, Brighton, Sussex-*doll kits, doll supplies, period doll clothes, hats, etc.*

Ridings Craft Co., 749 Bradford Road, Batley, West Yorks WF17 8HZ-*wigs and hair, hats, trimmings, feathers, doll kits*

Sunday Dolls, 7 Park Drive, East Sheen, London SW14 8RB-*doll kits, ribbons and trimmings, buttons, hats, accessories*

Vokings Fabrics, Worthing-*fabrics, tiny buttons and ribbons, fur fabrics*

FURTHER READING

Aitken, Leila, *Toys, Gifts and Decorations,* Dryad Press, London

Anderson, Enid, *Patterns for Soft Toys,* Batsford, London

Anderson, Enid, *Techniques of Soft Toy Making,* Batsford, London

Eaton, Faith, *Care and Repair of Antique and Modern Dolls,* Batsford, London

Greenhowe, Jean, *Dolls in National and Folk Costume,* Batsford, London

Greenhowe, Jean, *Jean Greenhowe's Miniature Toys,* Batsford, London

Greenhowe, Jean, *Making a Victorian Doll's House,* Batsford, London

Greenhowe, Jean, *Making Miniature Toys and Dolls,* Batsford, London

Greenhowe, Jean, *Making Mascot Dolls,* Batsford, London

Snook, Barbara, *Creative Soft Toys,* Dryad Press, London

Snook, Barbara, *Puppets,* Dryad Press, London

Wells, William, *Performing Wooden Toys,* Batsford, London

INDEX